Bread
On The Table

Baking Traditions for Today

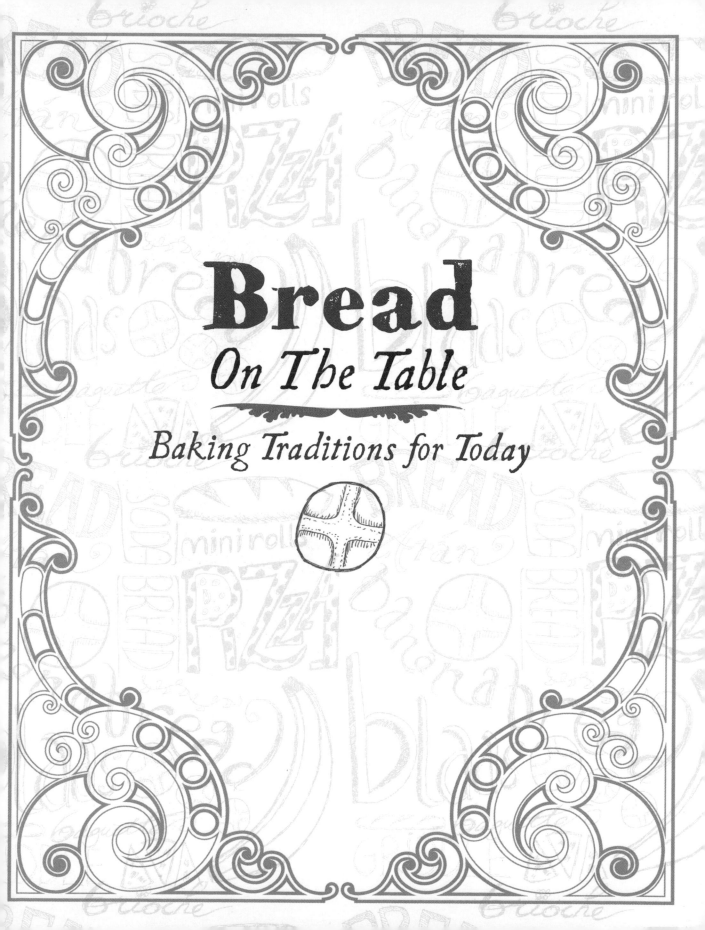

VALERIE O'CONNOR is a cook, food writer and photographer; she has worked in professional kitchens from Brussels to Malaysia. She is a qualified organic horticulturalist and tutors in food growing, cooking and baking. She is widely published in the press and has appeared as a guest critic on Masterchef Ireland.

breadbread

This book is dedicated to my Mum and Dad

Acknowledgements

This book was an epic project for me, one which I very much enjoyed and couldn't have done as well without the help and generosity of so many people: Leon & Saoirse O'Connor, my two boys and best critics. My brother Chris for his unending support. Billy Hayes, Dee MacMahon, Karen Morgan, Maggie Hanley, Verette O'Sullivan, Patricia Roberts, Eugene Ryan & family, Sean Molony, Bryan O'Brien, Laura Boland, Veitch & Mack Russell, Collette McMahon, John Flynn, Maria & Mason Harper, Caroline Rigney, Joe Fitzmaurice, Michael & Dermot Walsh, The Concannons of Inis Mór (Aran Islands), Vincent McCarron, basket weaver on Inis Mór, Paul Cosgrove, Peter Ward, Elizabeth Zollinger, Birgitta Curtin, Kevin Dundon, Fergus Finucane, Jim McNamara, Nicola Kennedy, Aoife Cox, Gaye Moore, Anne Marie Gleeson, Santosh Sivan, Patrick Ryan. I would like to thank The O'Brien Press for taking a chance on me. Last, but not least, I want to thank my sister Anne, who loved toast so much she buttered it twice, and whose short but vibrant life encourages me to keep striving for more in this one.

First published 2014 by
The O'Brien Press Ltd,
12 Terenure Road East, Rathgar,
Dublin 6, Ireland.
Tel: +353 1 4923333; Fax: +353 1 4922777
E-mail: books@obrien.ie.
Website: www.obrien.ie

ISBN: 978-1-84717-542-7

1 3 5 7 8 6 4 2
14 16 18 19 17 15

Printed by EDELVIVES, Spain
The paper in this book is produced using pulp from managed forests

Bread
On The Table

Baking Traditions for Today

VALERIE O'CONNOR

THE O'BRIEN PRESS
DUBLIN

Contents

Walk on the Wild Side

Gluten-Free Goodies GF

Sweet Things

Butter

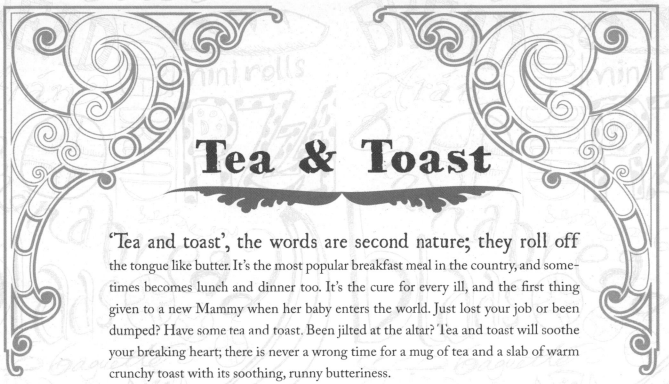

Tea & Toast

'Tea and toast', the words are second nature; they roll off the tongue like butter. It's the most popular breakfast meal in the country, and sometimes becomes lunch and dinner too. It's the cure for every ill, and the first thing given to a new Mammy when her baby enters the world. Just lost your job or been dumped? Have some tea and toast. Been jilted at the altar? Tea and toast will soothe your breaking heart; there is never a wrong time for a mug of tea and a slab of warm crunchy toast with its soothing, runny butteriness.

Walk into any Irish home and the first thing your host will do is put the kettle on, without asking, and assume that you want a cup of tea. You'll probably be asked if you want some toast. You might say 'no', but you'll have a slice if the butter, jam and honey are put on the table. You'll sit down and the chat will flow, problems will be shared or you'll just have a laugh about all the good stuff and some of the bad.

Toast is the blank canvas to the artist in all of us. Upon it you can paint your marmalade, jam, peanut butter, cheese, ham, beans, rashers, sausages, eggs, paté, mackerel, smoked salmon, chocolate spread, tinned spaghetti, scrambled eggs. Sexed up melba toast is served in restaurants with foie gras and salmon paté. Bruschetta is just toast with tomatoes and garlic. Toast with a runny egg is my breakfast of choice.

There is no better loaf to master in your own kitchen than the basic white. It's a bread you will come to know and love; it's made with yeast – which makes it rise – after that it's just flour, water and salt. You'll love it because of the feeling of excitement and satisfaction that comes with taking your first loaf from the oven; you'll feel proud, you'll smell it, and tap it to make sure it's done. It will make little crunchy noises all on its own as its hot crust hits the cool air. You'll wait maybe ten minutes to cut into the hot crunchiness, and slather real butter over the steaming slices. You, the proud baker, will watch your loaf disappear in minutes before your eyes.

Master this bread and you'll be baking bread rolls, burger buns, baguettes and pizzas, for this is the base for all those good things and will give you confidence as a bread baker.

White Yeast Breads

A Note on Yeast

Yeast occurs naturally in the air around us; yeast particles are everywhere. Once science figured out how to grow and multiply yeast it became possible to make it in large volumes and package and sell it. In the recipes that follow for yeast bread, I have given the measurements in grams, as that is how yeast is packaged and sold commercially.

There are three main types of yeast that you can bake with at home, it's an open debate as to the results from one or the other. There are no rules, just use what suits you, or try them all in your own time.

Fresh yeast: preferred by most real bread bakers this sweetly-pungent stuff comes in a block from good food shops or a kind baker might give you a slice. Keep it in the fridge and use it up quickly.

Fast-action yeast: comes in sachets measured for one loaf each. It's handy, readily available and works just fine.

Baker's yeast: also powdered, has a slightly stronger flavour and is easy to use.

Fresh yeast is usually added to bread by crumbling it in, while fast-action yeast can be sprinkled in. Depending on the recipe, yeast is often 'sponged' (added to water and allowed to froth up) before being added to the bread mix; baker's yeast is always sponged. (See 'Bread Lingo' on p 152 for more baking terminology.)

Basic White Bread

Ordinary yet special, with this dough you can do anything. It provides the backbone for many white bread recipes and it can be shaped in lots of ways, filled and flavoured with just about anything. Get this one right and you'll soon be making rolls, baguettes and pizzas.

Makes one loaf
Ingredients:
500g/1lb 2oz strong white flour
7g fast-action yeast or 15g fresh yeast
5g/1 tsp salt
350ml/12 floz tepid water
Oven 220C/430F/Gas 7
Prepare a 2lb loaf tin by greasing it well with butter or oil and grease a large board or table with a little oil for kneading the dough

1. Put the flour into a large bowl, crumble in the fresh yeast and rub it through the flour or sprinkle in the fast-action yeast (pics 1 & 2). Add the salt and pour in almost all of the water (pic 3). Bring everything together with your hand or a dough scraper until you have a craggy mess (pic 4).

2. Turn the mixture out onto an oiled work surface. Knead the dough for 10-12 minutes, resisting the temptation to flour it (pic 5). Get your hands under the mix and lift it up, slap it down and keep doing this until it starts to get smooth. It will seem unruly, but it will start to become elastic as you push and pull: this is the gluten being activated and developing that springy characteristic that yeast breads have. When it begins to become smooth you can lift it up and see if it will stretch easily

(pic 6).

3. If you hold it up to the light and stretch a piece you should be able to see the light and shadows through it; this is called the window-pane effect.

4. Shape it roughly into a ball (pic 7) and pop it back into the mixing bowl, cover it with a tea towel (or piece of cling film rubbed with a little oil) and place in a draught-free place for an hour. This time is called 'resting' the dough (pic 8).

5. After an hour the dough should have doubled in size and will leave an indent if you push into it with your finger. It gets exciting at this stage as you see your efforts paying off. Carefully scoop the dough out with your hand, put it on the table and firmly press it, folding it over itself a few times to push the air out and develop the gluten a bit more (pic 9 & 10). Pop the dough into the prepared tin and return it to its warm spot for another hour, again covered with a tea towel. This is the time that the dough 'proves' (pic 11).

6. Half an hour before baking time preheat the oven – it needs to be good and hot for bread. If you have a water sprayer have it handy as a spray or splash of water in the oven creates steam and gives a lovely crust to your loaf. Your dough should be pushing up the tea towel, eager to get into the oven to be baked. Carry it, like a precious prize, to the warm kitchen.

7. With a very sharp knife, swiftly slash a few lines into the top of your loaf. Pop the tin into the centre of the preheated oven, spray a few jets of water (or pour an egg-cup of water into the bottom tray of the oven). Bake the loaf for 40-50 minutes, depending on the temperament of your oven, until it is a nice, brown colour.

8. Take the loaf from the oven; it should tip out easily from its tin so that you can tap its bottom. If it sounds hollow, it's cooked. Put it back into the oven without the tin for a further five minutes to crisp up the crust all round. Cool it on a wire rack, or on top of the tin, until you can't wait any longer and just have to slice it. Have your butter at the ready and devour happily, little else will bring you so much pride in the kitchen.

Pic 1

Pic 2

Pic 3

Pic 4

Pic 5

Pic 6

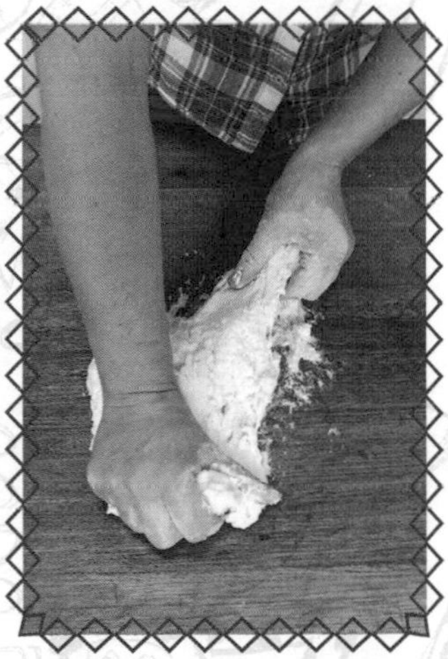

Pic 7

Pic 8

Pic 9

Pic 10

Pic 11

Pic 12

Mini Rolls

I bake these mini rolls in muffins tins, which gives them a really uniform size and shape – very professional! You can get creative by adding flavours like mixed seeds, or some cooled sautéed onions and sage.

Makes 24 mini rolls
Ingredients:
One batch of basic white yeast dough, rested, as per page 15
Poppy and sesame seeds, to sprinkle
Milk for brushing
Oven 200C/400F/Gas 6

1. Knock back the rested dough and cut it in two. Roll each piece out into a long sausage and then cut these in two. Continue dividing until you have twelve pieces from each half.
2. Roll each piece into a neat ball and pop them into the prepared muffin tins.
3. Return the rolls to a warm spot, covered lightly with tea towels, and leave to prove for a further 30 minutes. Meanwhile have the oven heating up.
4. Brush the top of the rolls with a little milk and sprinkle over some poppy or sesame seeds.
5. Pop the trays into the hot oven and spray or splash with water. Bake for 10-15 minutes until golden and crispy.

Burger Buns

How many burger buns do we eat as a nation? Packaged burger buns are laden with sugar, and additives, but making your own can easily become part of your bread-baking routine. You can double (or treble) your basic white bread quantity and make these at the same time as a loaf and freeze them. Their appearance can be as professional as if they came straight from a lovely traditional Irish bakery.

Makes 9 decent-sized rolls
Ingredients:
One batch basic white bread dough, rested, as per page 15
Flour for dusting
Oven 200C/375F/ Gas 6
Flour a 20x30cm/8x12inch baking tray

1. Once your dough has rested, turn it out onto a lightly-floured work surface and knock it back to get the air out. Cut the dough into three pieces, roll these loosely into sausages and cut each one into three again.

2. Roll each piece into a ball and place on the tray with space in between for rising. Press them down gently to flatten and cover with a tea towel, returning them to the warm spot for proving for a further 40 minutes or so.

3. When you return to get them, they will have doubled in size and be all snuggled together – this is a good thing!

4. Preheat the oven, then dust the rolls with flour; you can sprinkle it over them with your hand or use a sieve. Pop the tray in the oven (there's no need for water for a crust as you want them nice and soft) and bake for 15 minutes until they are golden.

They look so great coming out of the oven, and when you tear them apart you get that lovely, soft, doughy feel. Use these for burgers, or sandwiches, and of course they are great toasted for breakfast the next day.

Irish Breakfast Pizza

It's the full Irish, in your hand! The perfect morning-after breakfast where a fry-up meets fast food, but with the cheekiness of a take-away. Who doesn't secretly love pizza for breakfast? When the pizza is ready the egg yolk is still runny so it runs around and mingles with everything when you cut or bite into it. You can go as basic or as flash on the ingredients as you want, from shop-bought own-brand bacon and sausages to ethically-reared, free-range pork.

Makes two 14-inch pizzas or four 7-inch individual pizzas
Ingredients:
One batch of rested white yeast dough, page 15
Flour for rolling out the dough
50g/2oz tomato purée,
3-4 medium-sized fresh tomatoes, thickly sliced
6 cooked sausages, sliced about ½ inch thick
6 rashers streaky bacon, uncooked, cut into pieces
4oz/100g mushrooms, sliced
Eggs, 4 for the large pizza, 1 each for the small ones
Fresh parsley and olive oil to finish
Preheat the oven 220°C/450°F/Gas 7

1. Flour a work surface, tip the dough onto it, knock it back, then cut into 2 or 4 equal pieces; roll the pieces into balls and leave to prove again for 30 minutes.

2. Flatten the balls, then roll out the bases by teasing them out with your fingers, moving the dough around and sprinkling lightly with flour so that they don't stick, until you have the sizes that you want. Lay them on pizza or baking trays.

3. Spoon on the tomato purée and spread it with the back of a spoon. Lay on the tomato slices. Scatter on the rest of your toppings, except the eggs. Bake in the hot oven for 10 minutes.

4. Take the pizzas out of the oven, crack the eggs onto them, then return them to the oven for five minutes. Get them out of the oven, drizzle over a little olive oil and a sprinkle of fresh parsley and devour. May require a beer, or at least a mug of tea!

Baguettes

Purists who say these are not baguettes are right: the classic French stick can only be called a baguette if it's produced under certain conditions and contains the four ingredients of flour, yeast, water and salt. Other purists will wonder what a baguette recipe is doing in an Irish bread book. The answer is simple: the half-baked, frozen loaf we call 'baguette' and consume in vast quantities, isn't a baguette at all, so here's a recipe for something closer to a real baguette than you'll get in most shops. Go on, do it, you won't queue up at a deli counter for those 'baguettes' ever again.

Authentic baguettes call for French flour; these are made with more readily-available ingredients, but if you can get French flour, even better.

Makes 5 baguettes of 30-35cm/12-14 inches
(Ensure you have two baking trays that will fit this size)
Ingredients:
One quantity rested basic white bread dough as per page 15
Oven 230C/450F/Gas 8

1. Take the rested dough and tip it carefully onto the floured work surface (pic 1). Knock it back until you've taken the wind out of it. It will be a lovely light, airy dough at this stage. Roll it into a sausage (pic 2) and cut it into five equal pieces (pic 3). Roll and tuck these into balls and leave for 10 minutes to settle (pic 4).

2. Meanwhile prepare a large tray or baking sheet with a clean tea towel, which you have dusted generously with flour. Fold the towel into little ridges. This is where the baguettes will prove.

3. To shape the baguettes, take a round of dough, flour your hand and press your palm down on top to flatten the dough into an oval (pic 5). Fold over one side into the middle and press it (pic 6), then fold over the other side onto this. This creates a strong spine for the bread. Repeat this on the other rounds.

4. Now roll the shapes slowly into long pieces of dough to fit into the towel folds (pic 7). Flour the baguettes and cover them again with a lightly-oiled piece of cling film and return them to the warm spot for a

further 50-60 minutes. Turn on your oven half an hour before this final rise is complete.

5. Have a water sprayer or a cup of water to create steam in the oven at hand. With your unbaked baguettes at the ready, get your baking trays and very lightly oil them. Carefully tip the rolls out sideways onto the trays. When all the baguettes are on the trays, slice little cuts into their surfaces with a very sharp blade and pop them quickly into the oven. Spray the inside of the oven with water, or tip some into the tray in the bottom of the oven; you must keep the heat in so close the door quickly.

6. In the first 5 minutes of baking spray inside the oven twice more, this steam will create a delicious, shiny crust. Now leave them to bake for a further 15-20 minutes, resisting the temptation to peek.

7. Take them out of the oven, transfer them to a wire rack to cool (although they are unlikely to last more than five minutes). Baguettes are famous for a reason; they are so light and yet with such a robust and crusty crust with a delicious full flavour that comes from that one thing that we can't hurry – time.

Pic 1

Pic 2

Pic 3

Pic 4

Pic 5

Pic 6

Pic 7

Easy Overnight Spelt Bread

Spelt is gaining popularity as it's easier for people with wheat issues to digest; white spelt reacts well with yeast and results in a lovely, bouncy bread with plenty of air going through the dough. Spelt isn't too keen on being manhandled and responds well to being left to ferment overnight before it's turned into a dough. This means you only have to do one rise, which works well if you're pushed for time.

Makes one loaf
Ingredients:
7g/1½ tsp fast-acting yeast/15g fresh yeast
300ml/10floz tepid water
500g/1lb 2oz white spelt flour
5g/1 tsp salt
Oven 200C/400F/Gas 7
Prepare a 2lb loaf or round tin by greasing well with butter or oil

1. In a large bowl, sponge the yeast in the water for 10 minutes (let it froth up), add half the flour and mix to a batter, cover with cling film and leave overnight (or for at least 4 hours) in a draught-free spot.

2. Add the remaining flour and the salt and knead the dough for a maximum of five minutes (any longer and the gluten in the spelt will collapse) until it is stretchy and elastic.

3. Prepare your tin and shape the dough. Lay it in the tin and cover with a clean tea towel, return it to its warm spot and leave for a further 40 minutes or until the dough is almost touching the towel. Meanwhile turn the oven on at least 30 minutes before baking.

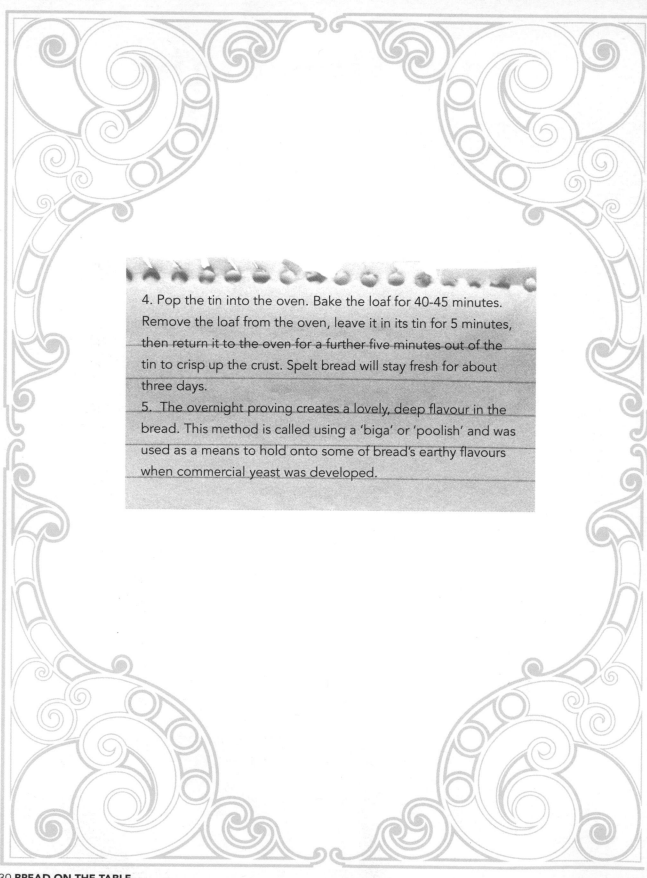

4. Pop the tin into the oven. Bake the loaf for 40-45 minutes. Remove the loaf from the oven, leave it in its tin for 5 minutes, then return it to the oven for a further five minutes out of the tin to crisp up the crust. Spelt bread will stay fresh for about three days.

5. The overnight proving creates a lovely, deep flavour in the bread. This method is called using a 'biga' or 'poolish' and was used as a means to hold onto some of bread's earthy flavours when commercial yeast was developed.

Blaas

'Blaas' are lovely floury baps, native to Waterford and parts of Kilkenny. The blaa is a legacy from the Huguenots who settled in the area in the 17th century. They traded heavily in wheat and developed the blaa, derived from the French word for white – '*blanc*' – as a means of using up leftover pieces of dough. The blaa is the only Irish bread under the PGI (Protected Geographic Integrity) seal, which means that only those produced within this region, using the age-old techniques, can be called blaas. These puffy, white rolls are usually bought in large batches, still clinging together in swathes.

The lovely blaa bakers, Dermot and Micheál Walsh, shared this recipe with me after a visit to their M&Ds bakery in Waterford city. Having spent three years as a student in Waterford sustained by these rolls it's a joy to be able to reproduce them at home.

Makes 24 blaas
Ingredients:
55g fresh yeast/3 x 7g sachets fast action yeast
570ml/1 pint water
1kg/2lb 2oz strong white bread flour
25g salt/5tsp salt
Oven 230C/450F/Gas 8

1. Sponge the yeast in 100ml tepid water to activate it, then top up to 570ml/1 pint with cold water; the ideal temperature is straight from the tap.

2. Make the dough by adding all the flour and the salt and bringing everything together into a craggy mess. Tip this out onto a floured work surface and knead well for 10-12 minutes. This is a stiffer dough so will really work your muscles! Leave the dough in a bowl, covered with a cloth, to rise for 2 hours.

3. Tip the dough out onto a floured table and knock it back to get most of the air bubbles out.

4. Cut the dough into equal pieces (you can do this by cutting it in 2 and then repeating the process until the dough has made 24 pieces, or you can use a digital weighing scales to portion off 65g/3oz pieces).

5. Roll each one of these into a little ball and leave them to prove again (preferably sitting in some flour), sprinkle with flour and leave covered for another 40-60 minutes.

6. This is a fun bit – take each ball and flatten it with the palm of your hand, it will deflate and you will hear it 'fart' a little. Place these flat pieces edge to edge, barely touching, on floured baking trays, sprinkle with flour again, cover and leave to prove one last time while the oven heats up.

7. Pop the trays into the hot oven, turn the heat down to 200C/400F/Gas 6 and bake for 20-25 minutes until they just barely change colour; they will remain mostly white due to the flour.

8. Enjoy these puffy, soft rolls while they are really fresh. I challenge you not to have to wipe the flour from your lips as you tuck in, knowing that you are bringing a little piece of Irish history back to life.

Tayto Blaa

When is a recipe not a recipe? When it's a Tayto blaa. Taytos are the most-loved crisp in Ireland and bringing a pack into an Irish pub abroad is known to cause a bit of a frenzy. The cheese & onion variety (salt & vinegar is too face-wincing for me) is my bar snack of choice. The Tayto blaa is a recognised regional speciality in Waterford – try it to believe it. Other popular fillings for blaas are a few crispy rashers of bacon, ham and sliced processed cheese or a local processed meat lovingly known as 'red lead'.

Makes 2 Tayto blaas
Ingredients:
2 blaas, as per p 33
1 pack Tayto Cheese & Onion Crisps
Butter, optional

1. Slice the blaa open horizontally. If you fancy some butter then butter it on both sides.

2. Pile as many Tayto as you can onto the bottom half of the blaa then swiftly and deftly (you don't want fallout) pop on the top half of the blaa. To make eating this easier, squish the blaa down with your hand and hear all the Taytos crunch together. Enjoy a real 'Irish food' experience.

Note: if you can't get your hands on blaas, then Tayto sandwiches on any white bread work equally well.

Potato Bread

Putting potatoes in bread works so well; it's something Irish people have always done, from potato cakes and farls to this beauty here – a classic white loaf. This loaf is much lighter than you'd expect and has a lovely springy texture. The toast is the best ever and the potatoes seem to keep it fresh for longer, not that it ever lasts long! There are often a few spuds left over from dinner and if you get into the habit of keeping the water – which adds to the starchiness and springiness of the bread – you'll have no excuse not to throw on a loaf of this. Try and get your hands on a nice, deep 2lb loaf tin, and you'll have a decent-sized, 'normal-looking' slice, perfect for sandwiches and to convert those who like packet 'bread'.

Makes one large loaf
Ingredients:
225g/8oz cold, boiled potatoes
600g/1lb 5oz strong white flour, or you can use a mix of white and wholemeal if you want a brown loaf
1x7g sachet fast-action yeast/15g fresh yeast
10g/2 tsp salt
225ml/8floz leftover potato water (or regular water)
Oven 220C/430F/Gas 7

1. In a large bowl, mash the potatoes, then add the flour, crumble or sprinkle in the yeast and the salt. Mix these together and add the water until you have a craggy dough, just like any normal white bread dough.
2. Tip it out onto the table. You may need to add a bit more flour to get a workable dough, so just keep doing that until it starts to come together.
3. Knead the dough for at least 10 minutes until it becomes smooth and elastic, then pop it into a clean, oiled bowl and cover with a tea towel or a piece of oiled cling film and set aside for an hour or until the dough has

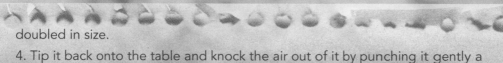

doubled in size.

4. Tip it back onto the table and knock the air out of it by punching it gently a few times. Prepare the tin by oiling or buttering the inside well and pop your dough into it, covering the tin with a tea towel. Preheat the oven.

5. After 30 minutes the dough should be risen, so put the tin in the centre of the oven and bake for 10 minutes before turning down the heat to 200C/400F/Gas 6 and baking for a further 30 minutes.

6. Check the loaf is done by tapping it on the bottom – if it sounds hollow, it's ready. Once it's out of its tin, you can put it back in the turned-off oven for a few minutes to ensure an all-over crispy crust.

7. Slice, slather with butter, make toast, make sandwiches and make it again and again!

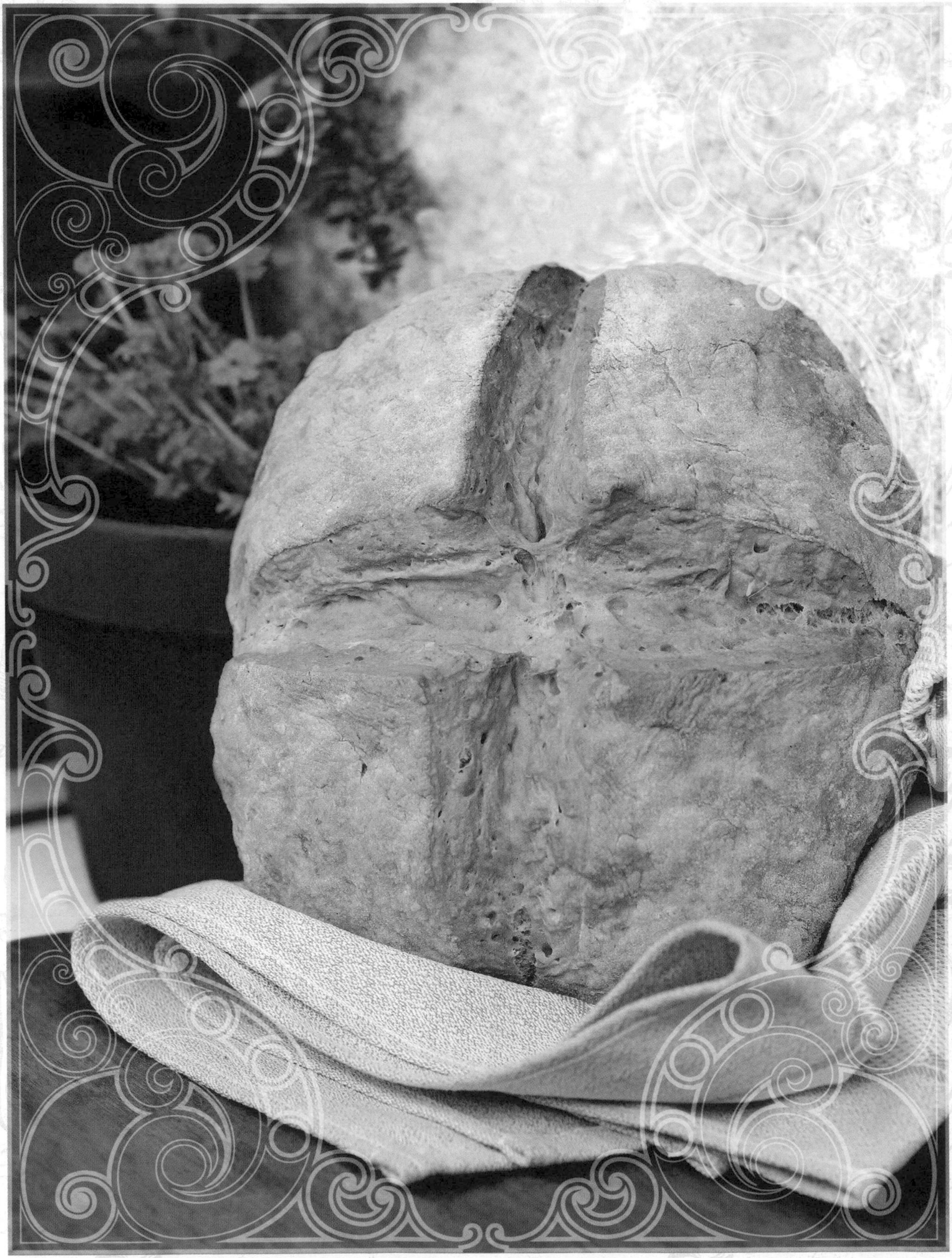

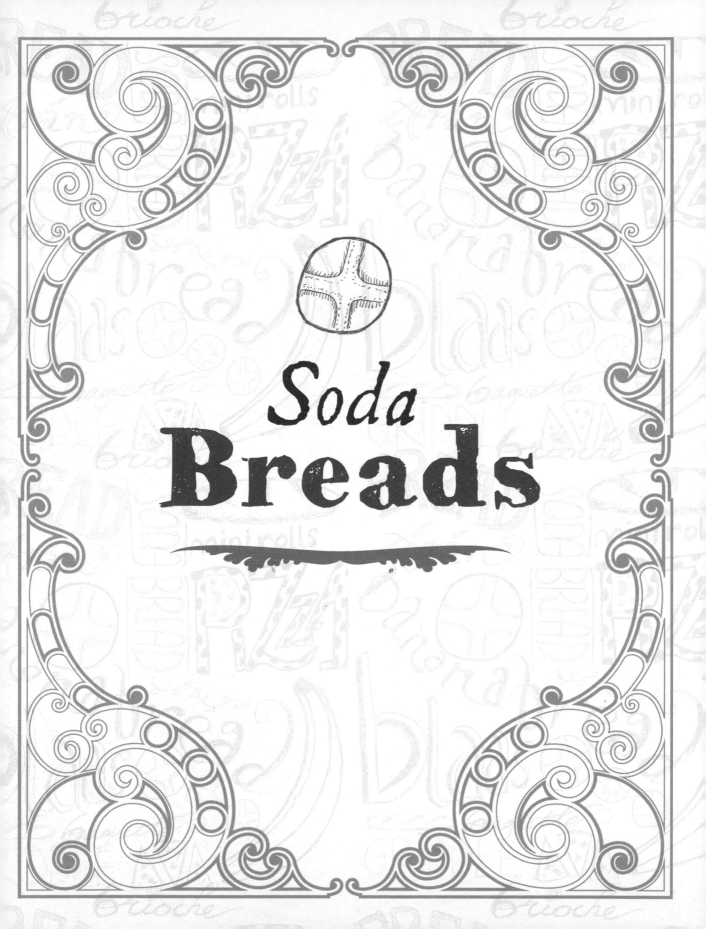

Soda Breads

White Soda Cake

The women of Thomondgate in Limerick were known to be great bakers and would leave their cakes of warm bread to cool on the windowsills of their kitchens; the more cakes you had cooling, the better off you were. Since then, people from the area are known as 'Soda-cakes'. Traditionally, the bread was baked over the fire in a cast-iron pot, but you can bake it in any standard oven. It takes literally minutes to throw together and the secret is simple: go easy, don't handle it too much. Use your hand like a claw to bring the few ingredients together and then you're done. The oven needs to be good and hot, as for all bread baking, so make sure you turn it on about half an hour before the bread is ready to go in.

Makes one cake/loaf
Ingredients:
5g/1 generous tsp bread soda
5g/1 tsp salt
600g/1lb 5oz plain flour or white spelt flour
400ml/14floz buttermilk, use real buttermilk leftover from butter-making
if you can get it
Preheat the oven to 200C/390F/Gas 6

1. In a large bowl mix the bread soda with the flour and salt.
2. Pour in the buttermilk and, using a claw-like action, bring the flour and buttermilk together until everything is combined and forms a wet ball.
3. Turn out onto a floured surface and, using a little more flour, gently shape the dough into a round, then flatten slightly with your hands. The raising agents will already be at work so if you press your thumb into the dough it should leave an impression.
4. Flour a large baking tray and carefully transfer the dough onto it (place your hand under the dough as you lift it to support it). With a large bread knife, cut a cross into the bread 'to let the fairies out' or let the dough expand.
5. Bake the bread in the preheated oven for 40-50 minutes until golden and hollow-sounding when the bottom is tapped.
6. Cool the bread by an airy window, or under a damp tea towel until it's just the right temperature to cut into thick slices and drown with butter. It's unlikely any will be left to go cold.

Griddle Cakes

These are also known as 'soda farls', depending on what part of the country you hail from, but the result remains the same. These 'instant breads' will answer any arguments you might have about not having time to bake bread, as you don't even have to bake them. You can make these on a standard frying pan with a good, heavy bottom on it. These are what I make in the morning when we've run out of bread and there's nothing for breakfast. Make these and within ten minutes you have warm, fresh, crusty bread, perfect for breakfast or for making your lunchtime sandwiches.

Makes 8 griddle cakes
Ingredients:
1 quantity of soda cake mix, p 43

1. Put your frying pan on the hob and heat to a medium to high heat. If your pan is too small to cook all the breads at once, simply do them in batches, or use 2 pans.

2. Tip your soda cake mix out onto a floured surface, sprinkle over some flour and knead the mixture for less than a minute, then shape it into a round. Move it round and use a little more flour as you go, pressing the round into a flat of about 25cm/10 inches. Cut it into wedge shapes with a knife.

3. Place the wedges onto the dry frying pan – there's no need to use oil or butter. Leave them to cook for 5-7 minutes and then check their colour underneath. They should be a nice, patchy golden to brown – a bit black is also okay. Using a knife, turn them over and cook for the same time on the other side. They will have puffed up nicely. I cook them on their sides too just to ensure they are well done.

4. Remove from the pan and slice open, enjoy with real butter, with cheese or jam, a big Irish breakfast, or all of the above!

Griddle cakes make the best rasher sandwiches: pack in a couple of slices of bacon and turn it into a BLT with some crispy lettuce leaves and slices of tomato.

5. You can use any leftover wedges as sandwich material for the kids' lunch-boxes: fill with any sandwich fillings, cut into pieces for dipping into hummus or use any way that takes your fancy.

Griddle-Cake Burger Buns

We consume as many burger buns as burgers and it's so easy to turn griddle cakes into nice, soft buns, perfect for holding a juicy burger and crunchy salady bits. Let the uncooked dough sit for five minutes before putting on the dry frying pan (this will let them puff up a bit before cooking). They will need to be cooked through fully so cook them on a medium heat until the bottom is nice and coloured before turning over. Keep them toasty in the oven while you cook your burgers.

Makes 4-6 large buns
Ingredients:
One quantity soda cake mixture as per page 43

1. Turn your soda cake mix out onto a floured surface and roll out the dough gently to about 1.5cm/½ inch thickness.
2. Heat up a frying pan to a medium temperature.
3. Get a wide rimmed mug, or a dough cutter, bigger than your proposed burger and dip the open end in some flour. Press onto the dough and repeat until the dough is used up, leave the buns to sit and puff up for about five minutes.
4. Cook these on the pan, without oil as you would the griddle cakes. You will need to do them in batches due to the round shape, keep going until they are all cooked, allowing the cooked ones to cool on a wire rack.
5. Fill these up with a juicy burger, some grilled chicken or a veggie burger, piled up with crispy, fresh salad and lots of ketchup and mayo.

Soda Bread Pizza

A revelation! This is the easiest thing since soda bread and gives you a perfect pizza in no time with little effort. You will need a rolling pin and a pizza tray. A batch of soda bread dough makes two medium-sized pizzas, if you only want one, then halve it. This combination of toppings is a take on the classic Italian Spinach and Gorgonzola. Of course you can use any toppings you like – go nuts.

Ingredients:

One batch of soda bread dough (page 43)
Tomato purée, or passata (this works best as it's easier to spread and not too runny)
100g/4oz Cashel Blue cheese, or similar
200g/7oz spinach washed and cooked, with the water squeezed
out and roughly chopped
Preheat the oven to 220C/425F/Gas 7

1. Cut the dough into two equal-sized pieces and roll each one into a ball.
2. Scatter some flour onto the table and roll out the dough into a circle to fit your pizza tray, moving it around bit by bit and flouring it lightly as you go, so that it doesn't stick to the table. The base will puff up in the oven so roll to a thickness of less than 1cm/½ inch.
3. Move the dough onto the tray, do the same with the second piece.
4. Bake the bases in the preheated oven for 5 minutes and take them out, this will stop them from getting soggy.
5. Spread some of the tomato purée or passata around and all over the base using the back of a spoon. Break up the spinach and cheese and scatter these over the base.
6. Bake in a preheated oven for 10-15 minutes until the cheese is golden and bubbling, remove from the oven and slice carefully.
7. You'll probably never order a take-away pizza again, so enjoy the savings as well as the satisfaction. Of course you can top these bases with your own favourite combinations, and you can freeze them too, perfect for emergency lazy dinners.

Wholemeal Soda Bread

Wholemeal soda bread is as classic an Irish food as you can get. It's easy to make, fast to get into the oven and requires no bread-baking skill to get right. While it is best eaten warm, it also makes a great base for smoked salmon or cheddar cheese – a snack that's fit for any occasion. The results you get depend on the type of flour that you use – a good-quality stoneground wholemeal will give you a lovely nutty texture and flavour. This recipe mixes half and half wholemeal and white, as a fully wholemeal loaf can be a bit heavy. Feel free to throw in a handful of porridge oats or wheatgerm.

Ingredients:

250g/9oz stoneground wholemeal flour, Ballybrado do an excellent one
250g/9oz plain white flour
1½ tsp bread soda
1 tsp salt
350ml-400ml/12-14floz buttermilk
Preheat the oven to 200C/390F/Gas 6

1. In a large bowl mix the flours with the bread soda and salt.

2. Pour in most of the buttermilk and mix with your hand in a claw-like shape to bring the ingredients together into a sticky ball. Don't handle it too much – some of the dough will stick to your hands, but just rub them together and it will come off.

3. Sprinkle some flour on the table and tip the dough out onto it. Knead it gently for a minute to bring it together into a ball and flatten the ball with your hand until it is about 6cm/2 inches deep

4. Place the dough onto a floured baking tray and cut a cross shape into it using a bread knife.

5. Bake in a preheated oven at 200C/400F/Gas 6 for the first 10 minutes, then reduce the temperature to 180C and bake for a further 30-40 minutes until the loaf is golden brown and sounds hollow when you tap it on its bottom.

6. Cool on a wire rack, traditionally the loaf was cooled standing on its side (pre wire rack days) and draped with a slightly dampened tea towel which resulted in a softer crust.

Boxty

'Boxty on the griddle, boxty on the pan, if you don't eat your boxty, you'll never get a man' - Irish proverb

Irish people from Sligo, Leitrim, Donegal and parts of Tipperary can be heard talking about boxty with much love and many a misty eye. The recipe for this easy potato bread came to me by way of Aoife Cox, author of the Daily Spud blog. She learned it from Leitrim native Mrs Rose McGirl who has been making boxty at home for years. Boxty is often cooked as pancakes, all crispy and bubbling, great with bacon and a fried egg, but the recipe here is for a boxty loaf baked in the oven – fitting for a book on bread. After the loaf is baked you let it cool, then slice it and fry the slices in butter and serve them in the same way you would a boxty pancake. The advantage of the loaf is that it keeps for a few days and is a filling and hearty snack. Unlike many boxty recipes, this one doesn't use mashed potatoes.

Ingredients:

1kg/ 2lb 2oz (roughly) peeled potatoes, roosters or pinks are good
300ml/10floz buttermilk
½ tsp bread soda
1 tbsp milk
150g/6oz plain flour (substitute this with white spelt or a gluten-free flour mix)
1 tsp/5g salt
A pinch of sugar
Preheat oven to 180C/350F/Gas 4
Prepare one 2lb loaf tin by buttering the insides well
You will need a clean tea towel, cloth or linen bag to squeeze the liquid from the spuds.

1. Grate the potatoes, then put them into a cloth or linen bag, or even an old, clean pillow case, and squeeze the liquid out vigorously until very little remains.

2. Pop the squeezed, grated spuds into a large bowl, quickly pour over the buttermilk and stir it in; this will stop the potatoes discolouring.

3. Mix the bread soda with the milk and stir this in to the potato mixture, then add the flour, salt and sugar, mixing well with a large spoon to combine.

4. Scoop the mixture into the loaf tin and smooth out the surface with the back of a spoon.

5. Bake in the oven for 60-65 minutes until the loaf is pale golden.

6. Leave this to cool fully in the tin before turning it out. Slice it the way you would slice cheese, rather than bread, by just pressing down on the knife. Fry the slices gently in butter until they are golden brown and delicious, top with anything from eggs and bacon to a sprinkling of sugar.

Seeded Soda Scones

Lots of people enjoy varied flours, seeds and flavours in their breads so I've added a few more textures and tastes to this version – add and subtract things as you fancy. These feel healthy so you can feel good about yourself (until you drown them in butter, cream and jam, of course!) They have a slight Christmassy feel from the spices (I worked on this recipe in December).

Makes 12-14 scones
Ingredients:
300g/10oz plain white flour (or white spelt flour)
150g/5oz stoneground wholemeal flour (I like Ballybrado coarse ground)
50g/2oz wheatgerm
100g/4oz mixed dried berries: raisins, cranberries or anything you like
2 tbsp each sunflower seeds and sesame seeds
½ tsp ground cinnamon and ginger
1 tsp bread soda,
1 tsp salt
300ml/½ pint buttermilk,
Milk for a milk wash
Preheat oven to 220C/425F/Gas 7

1. In a large bowl combine all the dry ingredients mixing them thoroughly with your hand.

2. Pour in the buttermilk, using your hand in a claw-like shape to bring all the ingredients together into a slightly sticky dough (depending on the flours you use, you may need to add more, or use less, buttermilk so hold a little back).

3. Tip the dough out onto a lightly floured surface and gently push it outwards until it is about 2cm/1 inch thick, or use a rolling pin, moving it about as you roll so it doesn't stick.

4. I always use a cup to cut out scones as it's so handy. Dip a cup or a cutter into flour and press into the dough, shaking it a bit to release the scone onto a floured baking tray.

5. Loosely gather the remaining dough and re-roll and cut again to use it up.

6. Brush the tops with milk and scatter over a few more seeds or leave plain.

7. Bake in a preheated oven for 10 mins at 220C/425F/Gas 7 and reduce the heat to 200C/400F/Gas 6 and bake for a further 10 mins. The high temperature helps to get a good rise on the scones. Enjoy these while they're still warm.

Easy Oat Bread

If you love the nutty taste of oats and the simplicity of a bread that you don't have to knead then this recipe is for you. It harks back to old flavours and is great with a hunk of cheddar cheese and a mug of tea. It's like porridge on the go – try it with sliced bananas and a drizzle of honey for breakfast, or take it work or school. If you don't eat wheat this is a great bread for you and it keeps for almost a week too. I've shared the recipe with quite a few people and everybody loves it.

Makes one 2lb loaf
Ingredients:
175g/6oz oatmeal
175g/6oz pinhead oatmeal
120g/4oz oat bran
1½ tsp bread soda/baking soda
1 tsp salt
600ml/1 pint buttermilk
25g/1oz butter, melted
Oven 180C/350F/Gas 4

1. Combine all the ingredients in a large bowl and mix well. Leave the mixture to soak for 30 minutes while you preheat the oven.
2. Grease or oil your loaf tin well and tip the bread mixture into it, sprinkle on a few more oats for a nice finish and bake in the oven for 1½ hours; the longer baking time is due to the wetness of the bread 'batter'.
3. Leave the bread to cool fully before cutting; this is a soft and crumbly bread, but so tasty.

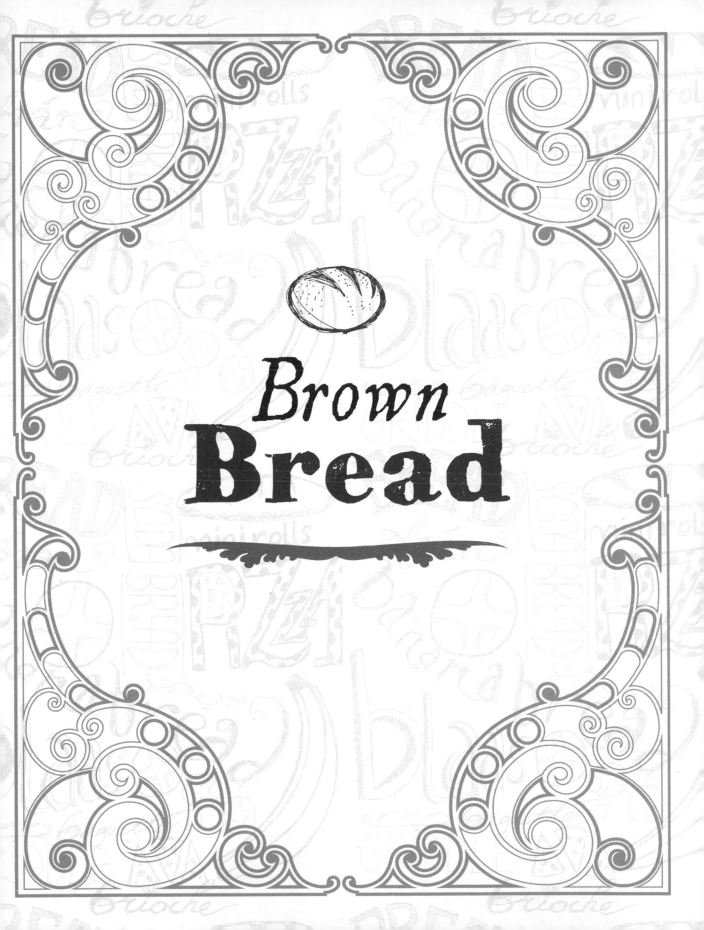

Brown Bread

No-Knead Spelt Bread

I bake this bread constantly at home and in my baking classes – it's so easy when you don't have to do any kneading. This is a great introduction to yeast breads as you get all the benefit of a good rise with none of the effort. This bread freezes really well, so if you'd like to make two loaves and freeze one, simply double everything.

Ingredients:

500ml/18floz tepid water
1 tsp honey
1½ tsp fast-action yeast
500g/18oz wholemeal spelt flour,
Approx 50g/2oz porridge oats
1 tsp salt,
2 tbsp mixed seeds
Preheat the oven to 200C/390F/Gas 6

1. In a jug measure 200ml/7floz hot water, dissolve the honey, then top up to 500ml/16floz with cold water, add the yeast and leave it to 'sponge' (froth up) for 10 minutes.

2. In a large bowl mix the spelt flour with the oats and salt, pour in the yeasty water and mix well to combine. The mixture will be wet and puffy, a bit like a thick porridge.

3. Spoon the mixture into the prepared tin, sprinkle the mixed seeds over the top, cover with a tea towel and leave aside for 40 mins to 1 hour until it has risen to just below the top of the tin.

Any warm, draught-free place is good for this. Have the oven preheating for 30 minutes before the loaf is due to go in.

4. Put the tin into the oven and bake at 200C/400F/Gas 6 for 10 minutes, then turn the temperature down to 180C/350F/Gas 4 and bake for a further 50 mins.

5. When the loaf is baked, remove from the oven and leave to cool in the tin for about 20 minutes. Run a knife around the inside of the tin, tip out the loaf and return it to the cooling oven to crisp up the crust.

Wholemeal & Honey Loaf

I also call this '3-2-1 bread' as it's so easy to remember the quantities that way. This is another effortless yeasty number that will have you brimming with confidence in the kitchen.

Makes one large loaf
Ingredients:
500ml/18floz tepid water
1 tbsp honey
15g fresh yeast/7g fast action yeast
300g/11oz coarse-ground wholemeal flour
200g/7oz plain white flour, or white spelt flour
100g/4oz rolled oats
1 tsp salt
1tbsp mixed seeds and rolled oats, for sprinkling
A little butter or oil, for greasing
Oven 200C/390F/Gas 6
Prepare a 2lb loaf tin by rubbing the insides with butter or oil

1. In a jug, dissolve the honey in the water and mix or crumble in the yeast, then leave to 'sponge' (froth up) for about 10 minutes.

2. In a large bowl mix the flours, oats and salt. Pour in the yeasty water, stir well to combine and spoon the mixture into the prepared tin. The mixture will be like a thick porridge at this stage.

3. Cover with a cloth or tea towel, then leave to rise in a draught-free place for an hour, or until the dough almost touches the cloth.

4. Preheat the oven for 30 minutes before baking, then sprinkle the seeds and oats on top and bake the bread for 55-60 minutes, leave it in the tin for 10 minutes before running a knife around the insides of the tin and gently tipping it out, then return your loaf to the oven for a further 5 minutes to crisp up the crust.

5. Leave to cool on a wire rack before cutting, enjoy with just about anything.

Brown Bread Nan Phádaí

Brown soda bread is an institution in Ireland, one that inspires heated discussion amongst (mostly) women about quantities and techniques; some folk like to add wheatgerm and oats, some throw in an egg or a glug of oil. I loved this bread from the first time I tasted it at the wonderful Tígh Nan Phádaí café on Inis Mór, the largest of the Aran Islands, where I was met by six of the eight Concannon sisters, all of whom had their own take on bread recipes. Their mother, who catered daily for her brood of twelve, baked three loaves of this every morning, along with another two cakes of white soda bread. If you think you don't have time to bake, think about Mrs Concannon! This bread is simply perfect, and another easy one. If you visit Inis Mór be sure to stop at the café and try this bread with one of their amazing salads.

Makes one large 2lb loaf
Ingredients:
700g/1lb 8oz wholemeal flour
1 tsp salt
2 tsp bread soda
100g/4oz wheatgerm
700ml/1 pint 6floz buttermilk
50ml/2floz sunflower oil
Preheat the oven to 190C/375F/Gas 5
Prepare a 2lb loaf tin by rubbing the insides with butter or oil

1. In a large bowl combine the flour with the salt, bread soda and wheatgerm, pour in the buttermilk and oil and mix with a spoon to a sloppy consistency.

2. Spoon the mixture into your prepared tin and bake in the oven for 55-60 minutes.

3. Leave the loaf to cool in the tin for 10 minutes, then remove from the tin and return it to the oven for a further 10 minutes. Allow to cool on a wire rack.

4. This loaf has a delicious, crumbly texture so take care when cutting it. It works with just about everything from smoked salmon to ham or cheese or just plain with butter.

Multiseed Flowerpot Loaves

Being a keen gardener with a yard full of terracotta pots, I thought it only right to include these cute flowerpot breads – featuring seeded bread, of course! I bake these breads in gardeners' terracotta pots. The pots must be seasoned for baking first: wash them in hot water, then dry them, oil them well and bake them in the oven at 150C/300F/Gas 2 for 30 minutes and leave them to cool. You can keep these pots for baking these cute loaves any time, and you can use any yeast dough. This recipe makes 3 small loaves in pots with an 8cm/3inch diameter.

Ingredients:
100g/3oz mixed seeds: sunflower, pumpkin, linseed, sesame
300g/11oz mixed grain or malthouse flour
200g/7oz strong white flour
1 tsp/ 5g salt
15g fresh yeast/7g fast-action dried yeast
330ml/10floz tepid water
Oven 200C/400F/Gas 6

1. Soak 60g of the seeds in some water, this helps make them digestible. Keep the rest aside for topping the breads.

2. Mix the flours and salt together in a large bowl, crumble in the fresh yeast or sprinkle over the fast action one. Pour in the tepid water and make your dough as usual by kneading the mixture on an oiled surface for 10 minutes until smooth and pliable.

3. Cover the dough with a cloth or tea towel and leave in the bowl to rise.

4. Oil and line the insides of the pots with baking parchment by cutting out small discs for the bases and long rectangles for the insides.

5. When the dough is risen, knock it back and sprinkle over the soaked seeds, kneading them until they are fully mixed in. Divide the dough into 3 and form 3 balls. Dip the top of each ball into a small bowl of water and then into the bowl of remaining seeds, place each ball – seeds upwards – into the pots, cover them with a cloth and leave to prove for a further 50 minutes; while they're proving, you can preheat the oven.

6.Bake the pots in the hot oven for 30 minutes; their smaller size means they will bake more quickly.

7. These look great on a dinner party table, especially one outside in summer, and make nice little round slices, perfect for patés. If you have smaller pots then bake them in the same way and give one to each guest.

Guinness, Treacle & Walnut Bread

A chef friend, Paul Cosgrove, gave me this recipe; I'd tried many times to get a recipe that highlighted the characteristics of our favourite pint, and this is a great one. Guinness works best in a yeast bread, making the most of the malted flavours and the brewer's yeast that make up this wonderful stout. The treacle brings out the typical burnt-barley taste of the brew and the walnuts give a lovely sweet little crunch. This bread tastes great with a big slab of mature cheddar and a pint of Guinness, naturally!

Makes one large loaf
Ingredients:
200g/7oz coarse ground wholemeal flour (I like Ballybrado best)
300g/10oz strong white flour
5g/1tsp salt
15g fresh yeast/7g fast-action yeast
2 tbsp treacle
300ml/10floz Guinness – from a can, bottle or draught
50g/2oz walnuts, chopped
Oven 200C/390F/Gas 6

1. Put the flours and salt in a large bowl and either rub in the fresh yeast or sprinkle over the fast-action yeast. Then add the treacle and Guinness and begin to bring all the ingredients together with your hand, or a dough scraper.

2. When you have a craggy dough, tip it out onto an oiled surface and knead it for 10-12 minutes, or do the kneading in a mixer, but finish it by hand so you know the feel of your dough. Sprinkle over the walnuts and keep kneading until they are fully incorporated.

3. Put the dough in a bowl, cover it with clingfilm or a tea towel and allow it to double in size for at least an hour.

4. Knock back the dough by punching it down and folding it over a few times. Shape it into a round and lay it

on a floured or oiled baking tray, covered with a cloth. Leave to rise again for 50-60 minutes, meanwhile preheat the oven for 30 minutes before baking.

5. Slice a few long cuts into the loaf with a bread knife or blade. Bake for 20 minutes and then turn the oven down to 180C/350F/Gas 5 for a further 20-30 minutes, checking to see if the loaf is baked by tapping it on its bottom, if it sounds hollow, it's cooked.

6. This bread has a lovely robustness and is very satisfying to bake.

Rye & Poppyseed Wedges

This is the most impressive quick and easy bread you can make. Rye flour gives a deep, earthy flavour, while the butter and milk in the dough make this into a lovely, sconey, crumbly treat. I prefer to use white spelt flour, but you can just as easily use plain white.

Ingredients:

225g/8oz white spelt or plain flour
125g/5oz rye flour
½ tsp bread soda
2 tsp baking powder
1tsp/5g salt
25g/1oz chilled butter
3 tsp poppy seeds
250ml/8floz milk
Preheat the oven to 220C/425F/Gas 7

1. In a large bowl mix the flours, bread soda and baking powder and mix in the salt.
2. Rub in the butter until the mixture resembles fine breadcrumbs, then mix in most of the poppy seeds.
3. Pour in most of the milk and, using a knife, bring the mixture together.
4. Tip the mixture onto a floured surface and gently knead it just to bring it all together. Form it into a round shape and gently press it down to a round of about 1inch/2½ cm thick.
5. Place the loaf on a well-floured baking tray, or one lined with parchment, and cut deep into it to create wedges, brush with a little milk and sprinkle over more poppy seeds.
6. Bake in a hot oven for 25-30 minutes until risen and golden.
7. This is best eaten while still warm so don't wait around.

Bastible Bread - the original sourdough

The 'bastible' was the big, black pot that was used to cook everything over the open fire in an Irish farmhouse. If a farm had cows, their milk was used to make butter; the liquid left over was buttermilk, which was either drunk or used to make bread. Most houses would grind a small amount of wheat and mix it with the buttermilk. This mixture was left to ferment and swell overnight and then baked over the embers of the fire in the morning, with some hot coals placed on the lid of the pot.

Once you've made your butter (page 146) you can use the buttermilk you have left to bake this bread, true Irish farmhouse style. As there is no raising agent of any kind, it will be quite dense. Alternatively you can use shop-bought, standard buttermilk.

Ingredients:

300g/10oz stoneground wholemeal flour
(you can mix some white with this if you want to lighten it)
1 tsp salt
200ml/7floz buttermilk
Oven 200C/390F/Gas 6
Prepare a small 1lb tin or use a small (20cm/8inch) casserole pot with a lid

1. In a bowl, mix the flour with the salt, pour in the buttermilk and mix it by hand until just combined. It should be like thick porridge.

2. Grease or butter your tin or pot well and tip the dough into it, smooth it down, cover and leave overnight somewhere warm.

3. In the morning preheat the oven and place the pot inside, leaving the lid on. If you use a tin, cover it with foil to seal it.

4. Bake for 30 minutes, remove the lid and bake for a further 10 minutes to crisp up the crust a little.

5. When the bread is baked, tip it out carefully and leave to cool before cutting. It's great with a slab of cheese and a big glass of milk, or buttermilk, of course!

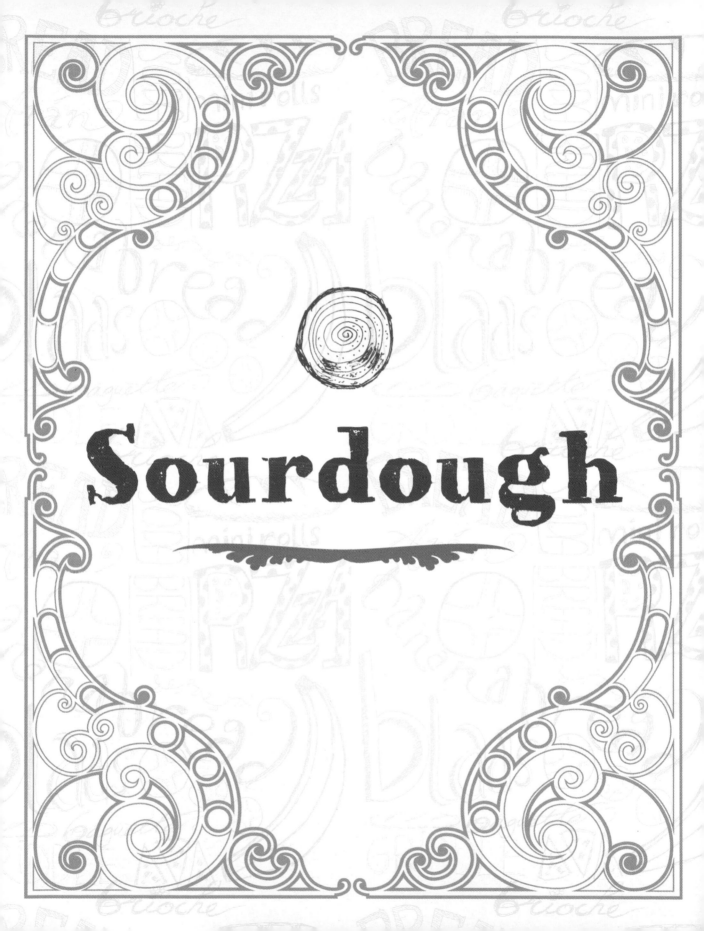

Sourdough

Sourdough Breads

The word 'sourdough' should be accompanied by angels singing and trumpets sounding! Baking sourdough breads has become so talked about amongst people who love good food that it's easy to buy into the belief that there's something cult-like about it, something mysterious. People talk in hushed tones about 'starters', they talk about feeding them like pets, they look serious, as if sourdough baking is a grave matter for darkened rooms and winter nights. Don't be put off by all this – it's just flour and water – once you try baking sourdough breads, you'll never want to stop. You may even find yourself thinking about it in the small hours.

The basics are easy, a starter is just flour and water mixed together and left for some time to ferment and grow its own yeast and 'pull in' natural yeasts from the air around it – it's magic! You can also delve into other worlds of starter-making like using potatoes and grapes, or elderflowers, or other things in nature that produce yeasts of their own; the world is your sourdough!

I can't deny the delight that comes from baking these breads, they are not time-consuming and are, in fact, quite resilient. The longer you leave your dough to prove, the better the flavour. I like sourdough to have a sourdough taste, some bakers like it to have a neutral flavor, but I don't see the point in that. Also, I love the taste and texture of rye flour so my best loaf is made using a strong white flour and a rye mix, 50/50; although this makes a sticky dough, if you use a mixer with a dough hook that's not a problem. Feel free to experiment, it's bread after all and while it may have a life of its own, I don't believe it has a mind of its own so there are no hard and fast rules.

I experimented at length, making starters from strong white flour, spelt and rye. Spelt and rye are both low gluten so need a boost from a strong white for the bread to develop a nice, robust crumb. Happily, as sourdough is a fermented food, it contains natural probiotics and as the flour is soaked for longer than regular bread, you will find it easier on your digestion and you are also feeding your good gut flora – it's win-win!

SOURDOUGH

Making Sourdough Starters

Joe Fitzmaurice of Cloughjordan Woodfired Bakery gave me the instructions for this sourdough starter method. He told me it would work, and he was right. He should know as he bakes a thousand loaves a week at his bakery in the amazing Eco Village in Cloughjordan. His breads are lovingly made and shaped by hand and baked in his self-built wood-fired oven.

Follow these instructions and you will have a loaf of good height, strength and lightness, and it's a real thrill when you do it all without added yeast. Organic, stoneground flour works best for sourdoughs as most of the bran is still in the grain and you're feeding the yeasts that are already there. Organic flour hasn't been treated with chemicals or pesticides and generally doesn't go through a bleaching process either. It's simple really; the better the flour, the better the bread. You can make starters using all manner of things from apples to potatoes; adding a spoonful of natural yogurt or kefir will give your starter a real boost. This method makes a traditional, dairy-free version.

Although Kilner jars are attractive, if your starter is very lively it might crack the sealed jar so a plastic tub may be better, you have been warned!

This recipe will make approximately 250g/9oz enough starter for one loaf.

Day 1

In a jar, bowl or tub with a plastic lid, mix 75g/2½ oz stoneground wholemeal flour with 75ml/ 2½flozs tepid water, stir well and leave covered for 2 days.

Day 3

Split your starter in 2 and discard the extra or use it up in pancakes or other breads. The reason for doing this is that you are diluting the starter and you don't want to end up with a bucket of it. There should be some life in the starter already, bubbles and a nice yeasty smell. Repeat what you did on day 1, stirring the starter well and leaving it covered for 2 more days.

Day 5

Repeat the process from day 3 again, noticing the life in the jar or bowl.

Day 7, 8 & 9

Add your strong white flour now – 75g/2½ oz flour and 75ml/ 2½flozs water each day for 3 days – and stir as before.

Day 10

Today's the day you can make your first sourdough loaf. You should have a nice yeasty, foamy starter to work with. You can use this starter to make a white loaf, a wholemeal or a rye. Over time you can experiment with different flours and combinations to find what you like most. Adding a tbsp probiotic yoghurt will give it a boost.

Once your starter is established, keep it in the fridge and feed it with 75g/2½ oz of flour and 75ml/ 2½flozs water at least once a week to keep it alive. (Feel free to give your starter a name!) When you want to make a loaf, take it out of the fridge and give it a feed for one or two days to bring it back to life. If it develops a grey-looking water on the top just pour it off and give it a god stir and a feed. Starters do die if neglected, you will know this if you sniff it and it offends you or smells like paint or a wet-dog. If this happens throw it out and start again. Otherwise, look after your starter and it will look after you with delicious loaves for years to come.

White Sourdough

You've grown your starter, now it's time to bake your first loaf, have fun!

Makes one 2lb loaf
Ingredients:
400g/14oz strong white flour, preferably organic
250g/9oz sourdough starter (it's best to weigh this for accuracy)
200ml/7floz water
7g salt
Oven 230C/450F/Gas 8

1. First make a 'poolish' by mixing the starter with the water and half the flour, cover this with a cloth and leave to stand at room temperature for 8 hours or overnight. It will be very lively and bubbly. Take a tbsp of this and feed it back to your starter jar.

2. In a large bowl, mix the remaining flour, the poolish, and the salt until you have a craggy dough.

3. Tip this out onto an oiled work surface and knead for 10-12 minutes until you have a dough that is smooth and elastic. You can use the 'window pane' test to ensure it's fully kneaded – cut off a piece, oil your hands to make the dough pliable, and hold it up to the light to see if it will stretch thinly without breaking.

4. Put the dough into an oiled bowl, cover with a tea towel or oiled cling-film and leave aside in a draught-free place (somewhere warm like an airing cupboard) to rest for 4-6 hours until doubled in size.

5. Line a bowl with a clean tea towel, then cover the towel liberally with flour. Tip the dough out onto a lightly-floured work surface and knead gently to get the gluten going again, then put it into the towel-lined bowl and leave to rise again for a minimum of 3 hours. Alternatively you can leave your loaf to rise in a tin or a 'ban-netonne' (proving basket).

6. Preheat your oven for at least 30 minutes with a baking tray heating up inside. Now carefully tip your dough onto the hot baking tray and make some cuts into the dough using a sharp blade.

7. Pop it quickly into the oven and

pour some cold water into a tray in the bottom of the oven, or spray the insides of the oven quickly with water to create steam. (If you are baking your bread in a tin, just pop the tin in the oven then proceed with the water.)

8.Bake the loaf at this temperature for 20 minutes and then turn down the temperature to 200C/390F/Gas 6 and bake for a further 20 minutes until your loaf takes on an appetising brown colour – the darker the better. Tap its bottom to ensure it is baked. .

Note: For the second proving you can shape your dough into its basket or tin and leave it overnight in the fridge, this will improve the flavour. In the morning heat up your oven and have the bread come back to room temperature for about 1 1/2 hours before baking.

Rye Sourdough

Rye flour has a delicious and distinct flavour and makes a lovely chewy loaf. As it is a low-gluten flour it benefits from the addition of wheat to give it strength and body to rise; you can increase the percentages of rye that you want to use as time goes by. It's wiser to make a fully rye sourdough in a loaf tin rather than as a free-form loaf as it needs the support of the tin around it. The loaf in the picture was proved in a 'bannetonne' or proving basket, which gives the lovely circular patterns.

Makes one 2lb loaf
Ingredients:
200g/7oz organic strong white flour
200g/7oz organic rye flour
240g/8oz rye sourdough starter
200ml/7floz water
7g salt
Oven 230C/450F/Gas 8

1. Follow the instructions as per the white sourdough (page 80), but this will be a stickier dough so it might be better to use a mixer for this one if you have it, if not, just persist with the kneading, the dough will come together.

2. Rye sourdough keeps well for almost a week and tastes amazing with pickled herrings or smoked salmon, as well as cheese of course. It's almost a meal in itself.

Potato & Rye Semi-Sourdough with Molasses

I love this bread – I love it so much that when I bake it I give it away in very small quantities, just a few slices here and there. If you've got into the habit of making some breads that take a little more time and attention, then you will love baking this one. It's simply loaded with flavours, from the rye to the molasses, yet has the lightest feel and the mightiest, chewiest crust. Big claims for a simple loaf of bread? You just have to try it to find out. It's a bit of a cheats' sourdough, using some rye starter as well as yeast so you don't have to take so long over it. If you're having spuds for dinner then cook a few extra and keep the potato water back to make the dough.

Makes one 2lb loaf
Ingredients:
200g/7oz cooked potatoes, roughly chopped
300ml/10floz potato water
250g/9oz strong white flour
150g/5oz rye flour
50g/2oz rye starter
15g fresh yeast/7g sachet fast-action yeast
2 tsp salt
2 tbsp molasses or treacle
50g/2oz sunflower seeds that have been soaked in water for at least an hour
Oven 220C/430F/Gas 7
Prepare a 2lb loaf tin by rubbing the inside with butter or oil

1. Set aside a few sunflower seeds for sprinkling, then put everything into the mixing bowl of your mixer and, using the dough hook, mix it on a low setting for 10-12 minutes to make a sticky dough. If you don't have a free-standing mixer, mix everything in a large bowl and knead as normal, though your hands will get very sticky. Flour the dough and get it into a manageable ball.

2. Leave it in the bowl, covered, for at least an hour, or 3 hours maximum. Then give the dough a good stir with a dough scraper or large spoon until it deflates a bit; it will still be sticky. Tip it into your prepared tin and sprinkle with the sunflower seeds. Cover and leave to rise for another hour while your oven heats up.

3. Bake the loaf for 1 hour 20 minutes until you have a nice dark crust. This may seem like a long bake, but as the dough is wet, it needs the extra time to bake through.

4. This bread keeps well for a week and improves with age – enjoy every crumb!

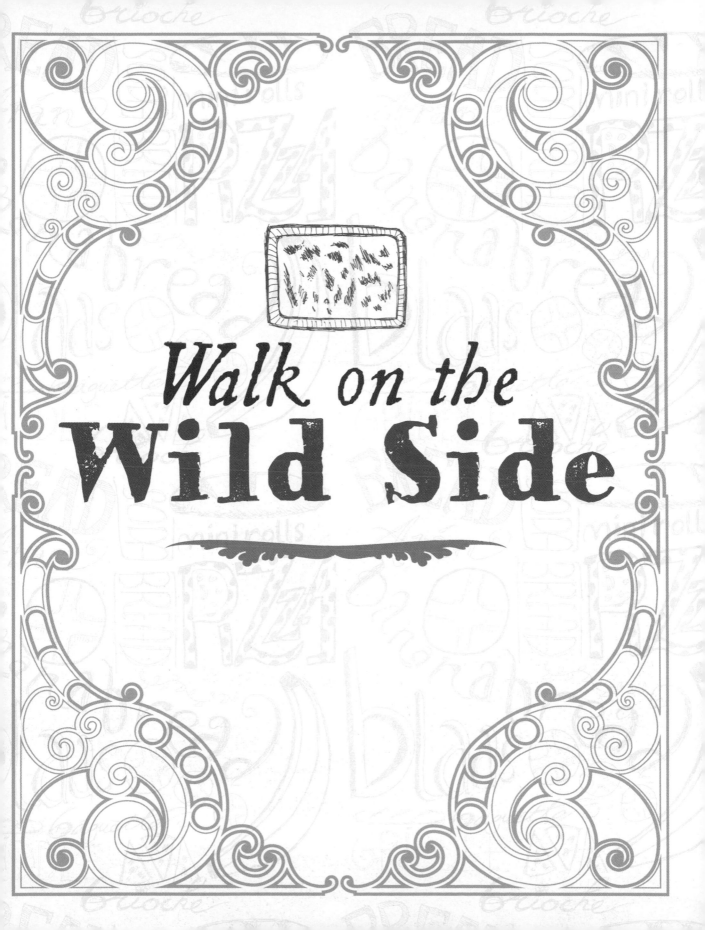

Walk on the Wild Side

Carrot & Dilisk Loaf

Happily, seaweed is making its way back into Irish diets. With the huge number of edible seaweeds available for harvesting on the west coast of Ireland, not to avail of this magnificent free gift of nature would be madness. I spent a few days on Inis Mór on the seaweed beds with Mairtín Concannon who kindly showed me some of the many varieties we can eat; naturally I helped myself and got busy in the kitchen turning it into even tastier breads. This recipe comes via Jim Morrissey who wrote *A Guide to Commercially Important Seaweeds on the Irish Coast*. It's a simple 'mix everything up in a bowl' bread and is devastatingly yummy.

Ingredients:

25g/1oz dried dilisk, soaked in water for 10 minutes and all the water squeezed out
(keep back some of the 'soak water' for later)
100g/4oz butter, melted
4 eggs
1 large carrot, grated
Pinch sea salt
250g/9oz plain white or spelt flour
1½tsp baking powder
Preheat oven to 190C/375F/Gas 5
Prepare a 1½lb loaf tin

1. Finely chop the dilisk (the easiest way to do this is with a mezza luna).
2. In a large bowl, combine everything and stir well to ensure there are no lumps in the flour. Add a little soak water from the dilisk if it seems too dry – it should look like cake batter.
3. Pour into a greased loaf tin and bake for 50-55 mins, cool on a wire rack and enjoy your taste of the sea.

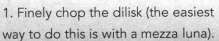

Sea Lettuce 'Baguettíní'

Glasán or 'sea lettuce' is a bright green seaweed that can often be seen covering rocks; it's super slippery, hangs in sheets and looks a lot like butterhead lettuce when picked. It's delicious used in omelettes or sushi, but you can also add it to many breads; it needs a white dough so it doesn't get lost in the bread. You can incorporate it into a white yeast dough or a baguette, a soda bread or even a scone. Here I've used an easy-to-work-with white yeast dough to make nice little rolls with the seaweed's lovely light flavour coming through.

Makes 6 'baguettíní'
Ingredients:
1 batch white yeast dough (page 15) rested to step 3
20g sea lettuce, rehydrated in water for 10 minutes with the water squeezed out and the seaweed finely chopped
Oven 220C/425F/Gas 7

1.Tip the dough onto an oiled work surface and knock it back by folding it over and pushing it down a few times.
2.Squeeze the seaweed to get rid of the water, chop it finely, then sprinkle it over the dough and work it in by kneading the dough again for a few minutes. Divide the dough into 6 equal pieces and roll them into balls, then leave them to prove for 10 minutes.
3.Take each ball and flatten it with the palm of your hand, fold over one side into the middle, press it down, then fold over the opposite side and press it down too, so that you have a strong 'spine'. Roll the roll out from the centre outwards using your hands, fanned out, until the rolls are about 26cm/10 inches long, then follow the instructions for making baguettes on page 25-26.
4.On a large baking tray lay a cloth that you have sprinkled generously with flour, place the baguette on it and make a crease to lay the next

one, repeat this process until the dough is used up. Cover these with a tea towel while the oven heats up to 220C/425F/Gas 7.

(see pics p 27).

5. Tip the rolls gently out onto two baking trays and make some cuts into the dough with a razor blade or sharp knife to help them open up. Place them in the hot oven and spray inside the oven with water, or pour some cold water into a tray in the bottom of the oven.

6. Bake for 20-25 minutes until they are golden brown and super-crusty.

Nori & Goats' Cheese Bread Sticks

Bread sticks – just waiting to be dunked into your favourite olive oil or guacamole, or chewed on while enjoying a big glass of wine – make a handy nibble at any kind of party.

You can let your imagination go mad here; with a white yeast bread as a base there's no end to what you can do, try brown sugar and cinnamon for a dessert-y bread stick to be dipped into a chocolate sauce, or an Italian version with chopped olives and herbs.

I'm using nori seaweed, harvested at Spanish Point, one of the most beautiful beaches on the west coast and a place where I've spent many happy days and enjoyed hefty picnics, not to mention rain and storms! The saltiness of the nori goes perfectly with the local St Tola goats' cheese filling.

Makes 24
Ingredients:
1 quantity white yeast dough (page 15), rested for 1 hour
10g dried and crumbled nori seaweed
100g/4oz St Tola or similarly tangy goats' cheese
Oven 200C/390F/Gas 6

1. Gently roll the dough out into a large rectangle about 1cm/½ inch thick.

2. Sprinkle on the seaweed and crumble on the goats' cheese.

3. Fold one third of the dough down onto itself and press it, now fold over the other side and press that down, like folding a letter. Firmly press the dough, then cut it into two pieces with a long knife and cut each piece into 12 long slices.

4. Twist the slices from either end and lay them on a floured baking tray;

they should take up about two trays.

5. Cover the sticks with clean tea towels and leave to prove for 20 minutes. Have your oven heating up and pop the trays in, along with a good glug of water into the bottom of the oven, or a spray onto the sides.

6. Bake in a hot oven for 15-20 minutes until golden.

7. If you want to make these ahead, bake them until pale gold and drizzle over some rapeseed oil before giving them a 5 minute blast in a hot oven just before you need them.

Spelt Soda Bread with Dilisk

Spelt has gained popularity in recent years, but it's actually one of the oldest grains on the planet. It doesn't take kindly to being handled too much, so soda bread suits it well. You can make it as you would any soda bread, but make sure that it's fully cooked as your bread will be more moist than the regular white. The best thing about spelt soda is that it keeps for a few days and makes great toast, the crust gets especially crispy in the toaster so slice it, toast it and drown it in butter.

Thanks to places like the Irish Seaweed Centre and people like Prannie Rhatigan, who is an expert in the health benefits and culinary uses of seaweed, we are seeing more seaweed on restaurant menus. This recipe uses much-loved dilisk, which is widely available from street vendors in Limerick and elsewhere in summer. You can also buy it dried and packaged in many good food shops or just harvest your own.

Ingredients:

500g/1lb 2oz white spelt flour
1 tsp salt
1 tsp bread soda
350ml/12floz buttermilk
10g dried dilisk, rehydrated in water for 10 minutes with the water squeezed out and the seaweed finely chopped
Preheat the oven to 200C/390F/Gas 6

1. Combine the dry ingredients in a large bowl and add the buttermilk, stir with your hand to make a rough dough. Next add the dilisk, mixing with your hand to combine. Turn the dough out onto a lightly-floured surface and knead for a minute and shape into a round, pressing it down to about 4cm/1½ inches in height.
2. Place the dough onto a floured baking tray and cut a deep cross into it. Bake for ten minutes at 200°C and

then reduce the heat to 180C/350F/ Gas 4 and bake for a further 30-40 minutes until the loaf is golden and the bottom sounds hollow when tapped. Leave to cool then slice and enjoy with a topping of smoked salmon, with a squeeze of lemon juice and a sprinkling of black pepper.

3. This loaf keeps surprisingly well, for up to a week. Maybe it's the seaweed that does the trick, but it makes it all the more appealing.

Wild Garlic Focaccia

Wild garlic grows prolifically in the months of April and May, scenting the air with a wonderful pungency. Curragh Chase forest park is laden with this lovely long, leafy herb that looks a lot like chubby grass. After I made wild garlic oil to preserve the garlic, I had to do something that would really show it off. I'd never really seen what all the fuss was about focaccia, but now I am converted. It's so soft and airy, one bite and it's true love.

Ingredients:

For the garlic oil:
Wild garlic (or regular garlic)
Olive oil
A little salt
Parsley, finely-chopped
For the focaccia:
500g/1lb 2oz strong white flour
15g fresh yeast/7g/1½ tsp fast-action yeast
300ml/12floz tepid water
50ml/2floz olive oil, plus extra for kneading and drizzling
2 tsp salt
Oven 220C/430F/Gas 7

1. To make the garlic oil, just blitz the wild garlic in the blender with olive oil until you have a nice runny consistency. If you don't have wild garlic, simply crush some regular garlic well with a bit of salt until it becomes a paste and then mix it with olive oil, adding finely-chopped parsley at the end.

2. To make the focaccia, crumble or sprinkle the yeast into the flour and mix in the water, oil and salt until combined. Turn out onto an oiled surface and knead well for 10-12

minutes until the dough is smooth and stretchy. Pop the dough into a bowl and cover with cling film and leave to rest in a draught-free place for an hour.

3. Get a Swiss roll tin, about 40x20cm/16x8inch (the exact dimensions aren't that important). Rub it all over with olive oil, pop the dough onto it and drizzle it with more olive oil.

4. Now push the dough gently with your fingers outwards towards the edges of the tin to cover the whole area. Cover with a tea towel and return it to its warm spot for 30 minutes.

5. Now have some fun gently poking little dents in the dough with your fingers, deep and straight down, but not breaking the dough. Leave it to rise again for about 20 minutes during which time you can heat up the oven.

6. Drizzle the garlic oil into the holes and over the surface of the dough, making sure you have little pools in places. Sprinkle over a last drizzle of olive oil and a liberal sprinkling of rock salt.

7. Bake in the hot oven for 20-25 minutes, leave to cool a little before fishing it out and tearing it apart like a flock of hungry seagulls.

8. Because this bread makes a nice big slab, it's perfect for a party and screams 'big glass of fruity red wine'.

Nettle Pesto Bread

Nettles are everywhere on this fine island of ours – free and abundant; we all have fond memories of falling into them as children and rubbing ourselves with dock leaves to ease the stings. But we can also do so many delicious things with our wild and wonderful free foods. Nettle soup in May is said to be great for the blood and contains more iron than a steak! Just be sure to go foraging in spring and early summer and cut only the top, young parts of the plants. This pesto also works well with the foccacia recipe on page 96.

Nettle pesto bread
Ingredients:
1 batch rested focaccia dough (page 96)
Nettle pesto
100g/3.5oz prepared nettles (cooked and chopped)
1 clove garlic
1 tsp salt
50g/2oz pinenuts (hold back a few for decoration)
100ml/3½ floz olive or Irish rapeseed oil
50g/2oz grated Parmesan or similar hard cheese
Salt & freshly-ground black pepper, optional
Oven 200C/390F/Gas 6

1. Handle nettles with care, using thick rubber gloves at all times until they are cooked. Wash the nettles and pop them into a pot of boiling water for 3-5 minutes to cook, by now the sting is gone so you can use your bare hands. Rinse them in a colander and squeeze out as much excess water as you can, then chop them finely.

2. In a food processor, or with a mortar and pestle, crush the garlic clove with a little salt, add the pinenuts and crush gently, stir in the olive oil and the nettles, add the cheese and stir well, maybe add a little more salt and black pepper.

For the loaf

1. Take your rested dough from its bowl and knock it back, gently easing out any air bubbles to give it a little boost. Spread it out into a rectangle with your fingers. Spread the pesto over the bread, leaving a gap of about 5cm/2inches from the edges. Next, lift up one side of the dough and roll it into a chubby loaf shape.

2. Pop the loaf into an oiled loaf tin and cover and leave to prove for another 40-60 minutes.
Bake in your preheated oven for 50 minutes until it's brown – and probably a bit green!

3. You can also treat this recipe like the Chocolate Swirls on page 122, cutting the log into slices and baking them as individual rolls. Pestos and flavoured oils can be used in so many ways with breads, as toppings for bruschettas, drizzled onto a pizza or anything that grabs you, it's robust and cheap to make and fun too.

Black Pudding & Apple Scones

Black pudding has rightly found its place on many fine dining menus and tastes great with many different accompaniments from apple to scallops. Its crumbly texture works well in a scone, as you can mix it in with the flour and butter crumb; in this scone, the apple gives it a nice sweetness. This tastes great with a tangy cheese and a pint, a meal in itself!

Makes 12
Ingredients:
400g/14oz plain flour
100g/3oz butter, chilled (I keep some in the freezer for this)
25g/1oz baking powder
150g/5oz black pudding (I love Curraghchase Black Pudding)
240ml/8floz milk
1 medium-sized eating apple,
1 egg, for egg wash
Preheat the oven to 200C/390F/Gas 6

1. In a large bowl rub the butter into the flour with your fingertips until you have light 'breadcrumbs', add the baking powder and mix lightly with your hand. Break up and crumble in the black pudding, mix it through.

2. Add the milk and mix with your hand or a spatula until you have a light dough. Grate the apple into a bowl and gently squeeze out any excess juice, mix it through quickly to avoid discolouration. The dough may turn an interesting purple colour from the black pudding, but that's ok.

3. Tip the dough out onto a floured surface and knead very lightly until you have a manageable ball, flatten this down slightly, cover and leave to rest in the fridge for 10-15 minutes.

4. Roll out the dough until you have a thickness of about 3cm/1 inch, cut into rounds and lay on a lightly-floured baking tray, brush with beaten egg and bake in the hot oven for 20 minutes until brown and well-risen.

5. These scones have a bit of a 'wow' factor and go great on a brunch table.

Smoked Salmon & Chive Muffins

These savoury muffins are so easy. They take about 5 minutes to get into the oven – perfect for a last-minute snack or as part of a bigger brunch menu. I use white spelt flour, but you can use regular white plain flour for this recipe too. Birgita Curtin from the Burren Smokehouse gave me the idea for these delicious treats.

Makes 12 muffins
Ingredients:
225g/8oz white flour
5g/1tsp bread soda
½tsp salt
100g/3oz chopped chives
1 egg
75ml/3.5floz melted butter
225ml/8floz buttermilk
125g/4oz smoked salmon, chopped
Preheat the oven to 180C/350F/Gas 4

1. Mix the flour, bread soda, salt and chives in a large bowl.

2. Mix the egg, melted butter and buttermilk in a jug. Pour the wet ingredients into the dry and mix quickly with a fork to combine.

3. Stir in the chopped salmon and mix lightly to distribute well.

4. Divide the mix between 12 well-buttered muffin cases and bake for 20 minutes.

5. Eat these warm as soon as they are baked, not that you'll need much convincing – and keep away from cats as mine ran off with one.

Gluten-Free
Goodies

GF

Nut Bread

This recipe was given to me by Dee MacMahon, whose family follow a grain-free diet. It's a little cake-y, and slightly sweet from the almonds and honey, but it's delicious and versatile. It's great for toasting and I love it with scrambled eggs for breakfast. As the almonds replace the flour, it's worth buying larger quantities of them if you can. The beauty of this is that it keeps well for at least a week when wrapped in foil, as well as being incredibly easy to make.

Ingredients:
3 eggs, duck or hen
1 tbsp runny honey
60g/2½ oz butter, melted
280g/10oz ground almonds
½ tsp bread soda
Oven 170C/325F/Gas 3
Prepare a 1lb loaf tin

1. In a medium-sized bowl mix the eggs with an electric mixer or a fork. Pour in the honey and melted butter and mix. Sprinkle in the almonds and bread soda and mix until combined, ensuring there are no lumps.

2. Turn into a well-oiled or buttered loaf tin and smooth out the surface with a knife.

3. Bake in a preheated oven for 40-45 minutes until golden brown. This bread doesn't need to be tapped to see if it's cooked. You can insert a cocktail stick into the centre and if it comes out dry, it's ready. Leave the bread to cool slightly in the tin, turn it out and enjoy with a good slather of butter.

Totally Tropical Banana Bread

GF

This is a variation on the nut bread from the previous recipe, but the addition of a few extra tastes and textures elevates this to a sweet, indulgent grain-free treat. The banana on top of the loaf takes on a lovely caramelly flavour, so be sure to have a piece on your own slice!

Ingredients:

200g/8oz ground almonds
80g/3oz dessicated coconut
½ tsp bread soda
2 large bananas, very ripe with black spots on the skin
60g/2oz butter, melted, leave a little extra for brushing
1 tbsp runny honey
2 eggs
1 tbsp light brown sugar
Preheat oven 170C/325F/Gas 3

1. Prepare a 1lb loaf tin by greasing it and lining it with baking parchment.

2. Mix the almonds, coconut and bread soda in a large bowl.

3. In another bowl, mash one of the bananas, pour in the melted butter and the runny honey, crack in the eggs and combine everything with a fork – no need for a mixer here.

4. Pour the eggy mixture into the dry ingredients and mix until well combined.

5. The mixture should now be like thick porridge. Scoop it into your prepared tin and smooth it down with a knife. Slice the second banana lengthways and lay it on top of the mixture, brush the banana with a little melted butter and sprinkle the brown sugar onto the top of the cake.

6. Bake in the preheated oven for 50 minutes, or until a cocktail stick inserted into the middle of the cake comes out clean.

7. Leave the loaf to cool for at least 30 minutes before turning out and cutting, enjoy warm with a tall glass of cold milk or a hot coffee.

Classic Scones

GF

Few things say 'welcome' like a plate of golden scones, all warm and sweet smelling.

This is a basic, easy recipe that once mastered can be changed – you can add cheese or raisins, spices or honey. Enjoy how simple it is! Scones don't need gluten as they are better when they have a crumbly texture; they work wonderfully well with ready-mixed gluten free white flour that you can get from any decent supermarket. Like all scones, these are best enjoyed fresh and warm, straight from the oven.

Ingredients:

500g/1lb 2oz self-raising gluten-free white flour mix
1½ tsp baking powder
Pinch salt
80g/3oz butter, chilled
320ml/11floz milk
Preheat the oven to 200C/390F/Gas 6

1. Sift the flour and baking powder into a large bowl, mix in the salt and grate or chop in the butter. Work lightly with your fingertips to combine it (see note opposite) with the flour and give you a lovely, light crumb.

2. Pour in most of the milk and, using a butter knife, cut through the mixture to combine the crumbs and milk until it begins to turn into clumps. Use more milk if it seems too dry.

3. Turn this out onto a gluten-free floured surface and bring the dough together with your hands. Press the dough into a round and get a cutter, or cup, to cut out your shapes.

4. Dip the cup or cutter into some flour and press it into the dough, lifting each piece and placing it onto a floured baking tray. Press any remaining dough together and use it all up. Brush the rounds with milk and bake in the hot oven for 15-20 minutes until they are risen and golden.

5. Split these open carefully and arrange them on a serving plate with bowls of cream and jam, a big pot of coffee and plenty of time for a long chat.

Note: as a child I made pastry a lot with my mother and learned the importance of rubbing the butter into the flour to get lovely airy 'breadcrumbs'. The easiest way to do this is to grate the butter into the flour using a grater with big holes, the size you would use for cheddar cheese. This stops you having to handle the butter too much and warming it up. Use your fingertips to lift up the flour and rub in the butter until it's combined into light crumbs.

Cheesy Chilli Cornbread

GF

This is an easy recipe that simply combines the wet ingredients with the dry, so you can make it in a good-sized blender or food processor. This cornbread uses chilli in the recipe and is great eaten warm with guacamole and salads; if you want to eat it with Chilli Con Carne, Mexican style, it might be better to omit the chilli. This keeps well for a few days and warms up well, also you can split a slice and toast it.

Ingredients:

1 x 300g can sweetcorn, drained

100g/4oz butter, melted

1 egg

250ml/9floz buttermilk

200g/7oz polenta

200g/7oz gluten-free plain flour blend

2 tsp baking powder

1 tsp salt

150g/5oz cheddar cheese grated

1 tsp dried chilli flakes or 1 red chilli, seeded and finely chopped (optional)

Preheat the oven 170C/325F/Gas 3

Line a square 20cm/8inch baking tin with parchment, or butter it well

1. Drain and rinse the corn in a strainer, tip it into the food processor bowl, blitz it well, then add the butter, egg and buttermilk and blitz. (You can also do this part in a blender.)

2. In a large bowl, mix all the dry ingredients except the cheese and the chilli. Pour the batter from the blender into the bowl and stir. Next, stir in most of the cheese (reserving a little for sprinkling on the top of the bread) and the chilli (if using).

3. Spread the mixture out in your prepared tin and smooth the top with a knife, sprinkle on the remaining cheese.

4. Bake in the oven for 40 minutes until golden and remove from the oven. Leave it to cool in the tin for about an hour to fully set; it will be moist and full of flavour.

Buckwheat Drop Scones

GF

Drop scones are made in a pan, like little pancakes, so they make a quick and easy snack and a great breakfast. Buckwheat is a godsend for anyone avoiding gluten; you won't feel that you are compromising. My youngest son, an avid pancake maker – and eater! – didn't notice any difference between these and ones made with regular flour. Whisking the egg whites separately results in a lovely light, puffy texture; they get their name from the mixture being 'dropped' onto the pan.

Makes about twenty drop scones
Ingredients:
3 medium eggs
300ml/10floz buttermilk
200g/7oz buckwheat flour
2 tsp baking powder
2 tbsp butter
Oven 100C/225F/Gas 1/4 (for keeping cooked pancakes warm)

1. Separate the egg whites from the yolks. Whisk the whites until stiff and set aside.
2. In a large bowl or blender mix the egg yolks with the buttermilk, add the buckwheat flour and baking powder. Fold the whisked egg whites into this mixture and break up any big puffs of egg white.
3. Melt some butter over a medium heat in a large frying pan and drop large spoonfuls of the batter mixture into it. Cook for about two minutes on one side until lots of tiny holes appear.

Flip over the drop scones using a spatula or palette knife, adding a little more butter to ensure the edges get nice and crispy. If you're making a lot of pancakes, you can have two pans going at once. Keep the cooked ones warm in the oven.
4. Stack up the pancakes and drizzle them in honey or maple syrup, or douse them in freshly-squeezed lemon juice and a hefty sprinkle of sugar, spread with jam or coulis, stack with fresh berries and yogurt, eat with crispy bacon – the options are endless!

Fruity Tea Bread

This is a good, old-fashioned tea bread, with the fruit soaked overnight in the tea to plump up and take on the flavours.

Ingredients:

150g dried mixed fruit – raisins, sultanas, cranberries, chopped apricots or a mixture of fruit, soaked overnight in 150ml hot tea.

200g/7oz gluten-free self-raising flour

100g/3.5oz soft brown sugar

1 medium carrot, grated

Zest of 1 lemon, grated

1 tsp mixed spice

2 tbsp butter, melted, or sunflower oil

1 egg

Preheat oven to 170C/340F/Gas 3

Prepare a 1½ lb loaf tin with butter or parchment

1. In a large bowl, mix the flour, sugar, grated carrot, lemon zest and mixed spice.

2. Mix the melted butter or oil and the egg into the fruit and tea mixture. Mix the wet ingredients into the dry and combine well with a large spoon.

3. Spoon the mixture into the prepared tin and bake in the oven for an hour, remove the loaf from the oven and leave it to cool in the tin.

4. Tea bread tastes great sliced and spread with butter and enjoyed with a nice cup of – yes – tea!

Spotted Dog

Not to be confused with 'Spotted Dick', a steamed pudding from the UK, this is the poshed-up version of soda bread that mothers would make on Sundays or special occasions by adding egg and sugar to soda bread and thus turning it into a sweet cake. This one uses a plain, gluten-free flour blend, which will result in a crumblier texture.

Ingredients:
500g/1lb 2oz plain, gluten-free flour mix
1 tsp bread soda, 1 tsp salt
50g/2oz caster sugar
100g/4oz raisins
300ml/½ pint buttermilk
1 large egg, whisked lightly
Preheat oven 200C/350F/Gas 5

1. Sift the flour, bread soda and salt into a large bowl, add the sugar and raisins and pour in most of the buttermilk, holding a little back in case the dough is too sticky, then add the egg.

2. Using your hand like a claw, bring the mixture together until it forms a soft dough, tip it out onto a surface lightly-floured with gluten-free flour. Gluten-free flour will not behave in the same way as regular flour, so don't expect the springiness that comes from baking with normal flour.

3. Form the dough into a round, pressing it together as you go and press it down to about 5cm/1½ inches in height.

4. Place the dough on a lightly-floured baking tray and slice a deep cross into it with a long knife, this will help it to bake through. You can, if you wish, poke each quarter with a fork as folklore dictates, to let the faeries out. Bake in the preheated oven for 40-50 minutes until it's golden and it sounds hollow when tapped on the bottom. To get a softer crust (as it can get quite hard), cool the bread under a clean tea towel that you dampen slightly by flinging a few handfuls of water at it.

5. Enjoy your gluten-free, traditional Irish Spotted Dog with butter, jam and cream.

Sweet Things

Chocolate Swirls

There's hardly a child – or an adult! – in the country who doesn't love chocolate spread. These chocolate swirls are sweet, but you could easily follow the same technique and fill them with a strong cheddar cheese and sautéed onions, or a mixture of dried, chopped fruit and nuts. Your kids will literally go nuts for these! I think they lasted about twenty minutes in our house. They're best eaten warm with a cold glass of milk

Ingredients:
One batch of rested white yeast dough (page 15)
½ 250g jar chocolate spread
Sugar for dusting
Oven 200C/390F/Gas 6

1. Once the dough has been rested, turn it out onto a lightly-floured work surface, knock it back a bit to get the air bubbles out and fold it over a few times.

2. Get a rolling pin and roll the dough, or gently pull it, into a roughly rectangular shape of about 20x30cm/8x12 inches.

3. Using a large knife, spread the chocolate spread onto the dough (if the spread is cold, warm the jar in a pot of hot water for a few minutes.)

4. Roll up the dough, lengthways, into a long sausage, like a long Swiss-Roll.

5. Cut it into two, then cut each piece into two again until you have 12 individual pieces.

6. Line a baking tray with baking parchment, set the rolls on it and then sprinkle them with sugar.

7. Cover with a tea towel and return them to their warm spot to prove for 30-40 minutes, meanwhile preheat the oven.

8. Bake the rolls for 15-20 minutes until they are golden and the chocolate is bubbling.

9. You can add chopped bananas and nuts to these if you want more flavours and textures.

Sally Lunns

These sweet, puffy little buns are native to Waterford and a legacy from the Huguenots who settled there in the 17th century. According to local bakers, these treats arc called 'Sally Lunns' after the sun and the moon (*soleil et lune*) due to their yellow hue (from the use of butter and eggs) and their dark side, provided by the addition of raisins. The bun is also popular in Wales, which also had a heavy presence of Huguenots; in Wales, legend has it that a young girl named Sally Lunn sold these buns on the streets of Bath, but the Waterford bakers claim the first explanation, which one you choose is up to you.

Makes 12-14 buns
Ingredients:
15g fresh yeast/7g fast action
200ml/7oz water
50ml/2floz milk
75g/3oz caster sugar
7g salt
500g/1lb 2oz strong white flour
1 egg
50g/2oz butter
100g/4oz raisins
For the sugar syrup:
100ml/4floz water
100ml/4floz sugar
Oven 200C/390F/Gas 6

1. Allow the yeast to 'sponge' (froth up) in the water for about 10 minutes, then warm the milk slightly and add it to the yeasty water along with the sugar, salt, flour, egg and butter and combine everything until you have a rough dough. Knead for about 10 minutes, until the dough is smooth and elastic, then add the raisins and knead again to combine. Cover the dough and leave in a draught-free place for an hour.

2. Turn the dough out onto a lightly-floured work surface and fold it over a few times to get some air out of it. Divide the dough in 2 and then divide each piece into 6 and roll them into tight little balls. Cover with a cloth and leave aside to rise for another 30-40 minutes.

3. Once they have risen, press your hand down gently on each ball until it flattens slightly, then lay the rounds side by side in a baking tin big enough to take them all (about 20x30cm/8x12inches), cover and leave to rise again for at least 30 minutes while you heat up the oven.

4. Bake the buns for 15-20 minutes until golden brown. Meanwhile make the sugar syrup by gently heating the sugar and water in a pot until the sugar is dissolved, and simmering for 2 minutes. Brush the buns with the syrup immediately they are out of the oven.

5. Split these open while still warm and spread with butter to enjoy a little bit of history.

Pic 1

Pic 2

Sweet Scones

As a baker you're nothing without a scone! It always seems to be one of those things that some people are naturally gifted at; the doorbell rings, an unexpected visitor arrives, the kettle goes on and a batch of freshly-baked scones is whipped up and baked by the time the cups and plates are laid out. I had to work at scones, to find a recipe that makes a lovely, crumbly crust and a soft, sweet inside. This one delivers on all counts.

Makes 12
Ingredients:
400g/14oz plain flour
100g/4oz butter, chilled (I usually keep some in the freezer for this)
100g/4oz caster sugar
25g/1oz baking powder
180g/6oz sultanas, or mixed fruit
180ml/6floz milk
80ml/3floz cream,
1 egg, for egg wash
Preheat the oven to 220C/425F/Gas 7
(The heat of the oven is crucial to the rise of the scone)

1. In a large bowl, rub the butter into the flour with your fingertips until it resembles light 'breadcrumbs', add the sugar, baking powder and fruit and mix lightly with your hand.
2. Add the milk and cream and mix with your hand or a spatula until you have a light dough.
3. Tip this out onto a floured surface and knead very lightly until you have a manageable ball, then flatten it down slightly, cover and leave to rest in a cool spot for 10-15 minutes.
4. Roll out the dough to a thickness of about 3cm/1½ inches, cut into squares or rounds and lay on a lightly-floured baking tray. Brush the rounds with beaten egg and bake in the hot oven for 10 minutes, then turn the temperature down to 200C/390F/Gas 6 for 10 minutes, or until golden brown and risen.
5. These taste fantastic drowned in butter, or go the extra mile and get some good jam and clotted cream.

Summer Pudding

Summer brings an abundant and delicious harvest of fresh berries, bursting with flavour and goodness. They're so tasty on their own as a snack, but this dish turns them into a real talking point, just by adding some leftover white bread and a little sweetness. Make this the day before you want to eat it so that all the flavours get to mingle really well, and the pudding is set and ready to eat. Frozen berries also work perfectly well so you can make this delicious dessert any time of year.

Ingredients:

750g/1lb 6oz fresh or frozen mixed berries, strawberries, blackberries, raspberries, redcurrants, blackcurrants

150g/5oz caster sugar

8-10 slices semi-stale white bread, crusts cut off

2 tbsp elderflower cordial (optional)

Fresh berries, to decorate

You will need one pudding bowl of 10cm/4inches diameter

1. Put the fruit and sugar in a saucepan and bring to a simmer, cook gently for 3-4 minutes, leave aside. Strain the fruit, keeping the juices.

2. Oil the insides of the pudding bowl and line it with clingfilm, leaving enough overlap to cover the top of the bowl. Cut a circle of bread to fit in the bottom of the bowl, then cut the rest of the bread slices in half. Dip the circle in the fruit juices and lay it in the bottom of the bowl. Continue lining the pudding bowl with the bread slices, laying them along the insides, overlapping them as you go.

3. Spoon the fruit into the centre and pour over any remaining fruit juice, and the cordial (if using).

4. Lay the remaining bread slices on top of the fruit to cover everything, ensuring there are no gaps.

5. Fold over the clingfilm, then get a small plate or saucer to fit on top of the bowl, and weigh it down with a tin of beans or something similar. Leave in the fridge overnight to set,

preferably on a larger plate to catch any juices that spill out.

6. Remove the plate from the top of the bowl and peel off the clingfilm. Turn the bowl upside-down onto a large plate or dish and lift off the pudding bowl. Peel off the clingfilm and decorate the pudding with fresh berries and drizzle over any remaining juices. Enjoy this summer delight with fresh cream or vanilla ice cream.

Tea & Coffee Brack

In Ireland, people traditionally eat Barmbrack at Halloween. 'Barmbrack' is a fruity yeast loaf that at Halloween has lucky and unlucky charms concealed in it. In our house, we waited with bated breath to see who would get them; the stick meant you would have an unhappy marriage, the coin signified imminent wealth, poverty would befall whoever got the rag – but everyone wanted the ring, which meant you would get married within the year, no matter your age or marital status! This version of brack is slightly lazier, as it's not made with yeast, but it's much tastier, and involves soaking the fruits overnight to plump them up and make them extra juicy. It has an extra twist – a drop of coffee – but you can leave this out if you like. Though quite rich, this tea bread is always served sliced and thickly covered with real butter.

Ingredients:

300g/10oz mixed dried fruits: raisins, sultanas, cranberries
300ml/10floz hot black tea and coffee in equal measures, or use all tea
300g/10oz white flour or white spelt
200g/7oz light brown sugar
1 tbsp baking powder
2 tsp mixed spice or cinnamon
1 egg
25g/1oz butter, melted
2 tbsp honey, to glaze
Oven 180C/350F/Gas 4

1. In a large bowl mix the fruits then pour in the hot tea and coffee and leave the fruit soaking overnight, or for at least 4-5 hours.

2. When the fruits are fully soaked, preheat the oven. Sieve the flour, baking powder, mixed spice or cinnamon and sugar into a large bowl, crack in the eggs and drizzle in the melted butter.

3. Give everything a good stir to mix it up and turn the mixture into the prepared tin.

4. Bake in the centre of the pre-heated oven for 1½ hours, checking that the top isn't burning (cover it loosely with tinfoil if it starts to burn).

5. Brush the cake with honey while it's still warm and allow to cool fully before slicing.

6. Wait for witches to call, or have a big slice with a nice cup of tea.

Brown Bread Ice Cream

This dessert became quite 'the thing' in fine dining restaurants in the 90s, and it's hard to understand why it disappeared from favour. It's an incredibly easy way to make an impressive and delicious treat and use up leftover brown bread. This works best with brown soda bread – Brown Bread Nan Phadaí (p 64) would be delicious because of its lovely nutty texture. You can go ahead and make your own vanilla ice cream as a base if you wish, but I just use my favourite shop-bought brand and mix it in. Cheating? Yes, but with results as easy and tasty as this who cares?

Makes 1 litre
Ingredients:
1litre/2pint tub good-quality vanilla ice cream
200g/7oz leftover brown bread, made into crumbs
100g/4oz caster sugar
Preheat the oven 180C/350F/Gas 4

1. Line a baking tray with baking parchment.
2. In a bowl, mix the breadcrumbs with the sugar and then spread them on the tray, put this in the oven and leave for 10 minutes, then take out the tray and give the crumbs a good mix around.
3. Repeat this every five minutes until the crumbs taste nice and crunchy, it will take about 30 minutes (they will be brown already so it's harder to tell from the colour), then tip them onto a plate to cool.
4. Allow the ice cream to soften at room temperature for about 15 minutes, then stir it up with a large spoon and sprinkle in most of the cooled crumbs, leaving some aside for extra crunch on top. When it's all fully mixed return the ice cream swiftly to its tub (you don't want it to be completely melted) and return to the freezer to harden. With its crunchy, cake-y chunks you don't need anything else with this, just a spoon.

Banana & Chocolate Bread & Butter Pudding

Bread and butter pudding re-emerged in recent years and is a popular choice even in fine dining restaurants where chefs love to get experimental with the flavours and serving techniques. Though it's traditionally made using raisins, there's no reason why you can't jazz it up with other combos that work well together, like this classic pairing of chocolate and banana. You need really ripe bananas for a good flavour, preferably with black spots on them, as they taste nice and boozey when cooked. This recipe transforms ordinary, everyday food into an indulgent, moan-inspiring dessert.

Serves 4
Ingredients:
300ml/10floz milk
1 vanilla pod or 1 tsp vanilla extract
3 eggs
50g/2oz caster sugar
100g/4oz butter
6-8 slices leftover white bread with crusts cut off
2 bananas
50g/2oz dark chocolate
Preheat oven 180C/350F/Gas 4
You will need a pudding or pie dish, not too deep,
about 20cm/10inches diameter.

1. In a saucepan, gently heat the milk with the vanilla pod or extract. Don't let it boil.

2. Turn off the heat and leave the pod to infuse for at least 10 minutes, then remove it.

3. Whisk the eggs with the sugar in a bowl and slowly add the infused milk to the mixture.

4. Butter the inside of the pudding dish well.

5. With softened butter, butter both sides of the bread slices and cut them into triangles. Layer the slices, overlapping, in the dish until all the bread is used up. Peel and slice the bananas and swiftly pop them in between random slices of layered bread – don't give them time to discolour.

6. Gently pour the egg and milk mixture over the bread and banana, taking care to cover as much surface as you can.

7. Grate the dark chocolate over the pudding and bake in the oven for 25-30 mins until it's nice and puffy.

8. Enjoy as it is or serve with some nice, cold vanilla ice cream.

Donuts

Who doesn't love donuts? Crunchy on the outside, bristling with sticky powdered sugar, almost too hot to handle, but who can wait? Take one bite into the paper-thin shell, crispy and sweet, then into the fluffy and puffy insides. Worth selling your soul to the devil for one? But one is never enough. Donuts are made from yeast dough, just like any regular bread, so the kneading technique is the same. This is a great one for a rainy day, they take time, but are fun and the results are so worth it.

Makes 16-20 donuts
Ingredients:
250ml full-fat milk

50g/2oz butter

500g/1lb 2oz strong white flour

15g fresh or 1x7g/1½ tsp sachet fast action yeast

50g/2oz caster sugar

5g/1tsp salt

2 medium eggs

Cooking oil, for frying

Caster sugar, for dredging

1. Have a pan ready to fry the donuts. A deep-frying pan is ideal as the oil needs to be about 7cm/2½ inches deep.

2. Gently heat the milk in a pan to around body temperature (if you test it with your finger it should feel neither hot nor cold), then add the butter and allow it to melt with the heat turned off.

3. In a large bowl, mix the yeast with the flour, sugar and salt, pour in the milk mix and the eggs. Knead as normal for 10-12 minutes until your dough is smooth and elastic. If using an electric mixer finish the kneading by hand.

4. Leave the dough to rise for 1 hour, until your finger leaves a dent in it when you press it.
Knock back the dough by folding it over a few times and punching it a

little. Shape it into a sausage. Cut the dough in 2 and then in 2 again and again until you have 16 pieces. Roll each one into a ball and leave to prove again on an oiled tray, covered with a cloth, for about 30 minutes.

5. Now heat up the oil for frying. Take each piece of dough and stick your finger in it, wriggling it around until you have a classic hole-in-the-donut shape.

6. You will know the oil is hot enough if you drop a piece of bread into it and it fizzles immediately.

7. Get a couple of large plates covered in kitchen paper and begin frying, pop the first donut in and let it get nice and brown before turning it over, lift it out with a slotted spoon and drain while you make the rest.

8. Now sprinkle lots of caster sugar into a large dish and dredge the donuts in it, covering them liberally on all surfaces. You can add some cinnamon to the sugar if you like.

9. Stuff your face with these beauties, you didn't go to all this effort for nothing!

Oatmeal Breakfast Muffins

Not only are these easy, they're also packed full of good stuff and have no added sugar. They freeze really well and make a perfect 'anytime, anywhere' snack. Feel free to substitute the white flour with white spelt as your taste or tummy dictates.

Makes 12 muffins
Ingredients:
250g/9oz rolled oats, the better the quality the better the results
50g bran
300ml/9floz milk, full-fat or skimmed, it's up to you
225g/8oz plain white or white spelt flour
1 tbsp baking powder
2 eggs
75g/3oz butter, melted
75g/3oz runny honey
1/2 tsp ground cinnamon
1 tsp vanilla extract
200g/7oz mixed dried fruit – any mix from raisins, sultanas, cranberries, dried chopped apricots
Preheat the oven 180C/350F/Gas 4

1. In a large bowl mix the oats with the bran and pour in the milk. Leave to soak for at least 20 minutes.
2. Meanwhile butter the muffin tin, or use paper muffin cases, taking care to also butter around the surface of the tin for the inevitable muffin-top.
3. Sieve the flour and baking powder into the oats and bran mixture and mix.
4. Add the eggs, butter, honey, vanilla, cinnamon and fruit to the bowl and stir well to combine. There is no need to use a mixer – it will just result in a tough bun.
5. Spoon the mixture into the muffin tin – really fill up the cases.
6. Bake for 20-25 minutes until golden brown and well-risen. Enjoy them warm for breakfast, slathered with more butter. These muffins keep well for about 3 days and freeze well.

Eggy Bread

What makes this really great is the use of your best white bread, either plain white yeast loaf or white potato bread. After that all you need is real butter, a decent egg or two and lashings of runny honey. However, feel free to pile on sliced bananas, fruit compote or whatever takes your fancy – this is a real breakfast treat. One decent-sized slice of bread will use up a whole egg easily. Gluten avoiders can make this using the nut bread on page 107.

Serves 4
Ingredients:
3-4 large eggs
½ tsp vanilla extract (optional)
25g/1oz butter
4 large slices of white bread
Honey, for drizzling

1. In a large, flat dish whisk up the eggs with a fork and add the vanilla, if using.

2. Heat up the butter in a large frying pan on a medium heat.

3. Dip each slice of bread into the beaten egg, one by one, turning them over to soak up the egg.

4. Lay a slice on the frying pan and let it cook until golden brown before turning to cook on the other side.

5. Drizzle with honey or your topping of choice; this is a 'stand up and fry while everybody else eats it up' kind of thing, like pancakes, good luck getting any for yourself!

Butter

Making Butter

What's the best thing to put on bread? Butter, of course! In Ireland, nature puts all that rain to good use by making delicious, lush, green pastures for all the lovely dairy cows to enjoy. This sweet, juicy grass makes the best milk and cream, which of course make the best butter. If you have a free-standing mixer, butter is so easy to make and it's a fun thing to do – a bit of magic in the kitchen. You can flavour the butter with all manner of herbs and seasonings. Watching the butter solids separate from the milk is very exciting – kids will love it. If you can't get your hands on butter pats, use two dough scrapers, or the best tools you have, your hands! You will need ice to keep the water very cold for rinsing and for keeping your hands nice and cool to handle the butter.

When the butter is made you can use the buttermilk to make bread, just as they did in the old Irish farmhouses.

Makes 2 small (170g) blocks
Ingredients:
1 litre/2pints fresh cream
2 tsp fine sea salt (optional)
A large bowl
Ice
You'll need: butter pats or dough scrapers for shaping
the butter, greaseproof paper

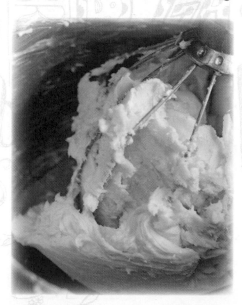

1. Pour the cream into the bowl of the mixer; it will need to have a large bowl as the cream almost doubles in volume as it whips. Turn on the mixer and mix on a medium speed with a balloon whisk attachment.

2. Keep an eye on the cream as it changes. It will become yellow and eggy-looking, then suddenly the fat solids will split from the buttermilk to form butter. At this stage the butter will look like well-cooked scrambled eggs.

3. Tip the butter into a clean sieve over a large bowl and squeeze out as much liquid (reserving the liquid for baking soda bread) as you can. Now wash it in the icy water, squeezing out as much buttermilk as you can. Repeat this process three times in clean water until the water is clear. Squeeze the butter as hard as you can to remove any remaining liquid, it should be quite stiff at this stage.

4. Spread the butter out on a board and sprinkle over the salt, if using, and work it in using the pats or scraper, until it's all incorporated. Shape the butter into little blocks and make any patterns you want in them, wrap them in greaseproof paper and keep them in the fridge, but not before you test some out on some piping hot toast, of course!

Flavoured Butters

Butter is a great base to flavour with many different things. You can simply chop some herbs and mix them in, or you can whip some brandy into your butter to serve with hot Christmas pudding, mix in some whiskey to serve on a steak, add cracked black pepper, chilli – the choice is endless. Once you've added your flavours, spoon the butter onto greaseproof paper or clingfilm and shape it into a log, then roll the butter up in the paper or clingfilm and twist up the ends so you have a nice, secure package that you can put in the fridge. You can also portion the butter into cute dishes to serve individually at the table.

Dilisk Butter

This is great to top a bowl of pasta or with grilled fish. Simply soak some dried dilisk in water for 10 minutes to rehydrate, squeeze out the excess water, chop the dilisk finely and mix it into the butter with a squeeze of lemon juice.

Mustard Butter

Mix in a spoon or two of a punchy wholegrain mustard and enjoy this one with pickled fish or in a ham sandwich.

Garlic & Parsley Butter

Crush a clove or two of garlic and mash this into the butter with some fresh, finely-chopped parsley. The parsley magically counteracts the after-effects of the garlic and looks great too.

Brandy Butter

Cream 150g/6oz butter with 100g/4oz icing sugar until smooth, slowly pour in 2 tbsp hot water and 3 tbsp brandy and beat again. Chill this sweet butter and melt it over hot mince pies or Christmas pudding.

Garlic Bread

Back in the 80s when Ireland discovered garlic, we were introduced to garlic bread as an accompaniment to lasagne, which was dish of the day at the time; garlic bread was 'the thing' and was served alongside pasta, pizza and even chips! Today, you can pick it up in the fridge or freezer at the supermarket, but it's so easy to make your own. It's also a handy way to use up semi-stale baguettes, rolls or any kind of white loaf – something magic seems to happen in the oven when you slather on the garlicky butter and the bread gets all crusty, hot and delicious, oozing with melted butter.

Makes enough butter for 2x12 inch baguettes
Ingredients:

3-4 cloves garlic, peeled, or 1 large bunch wild garlic, finely chopped
2 semi-stale baguettes or other suitable bread
100-200g/4-8oz butter, depending on how buttery you like things
20g/1oz fresh parsley
Squeeze of fresh lemon juice (optional, but delicious)
Preheat oven 200C/390F/Gas 6

1. The easiest way to peel a garlic clove is to put it on a chopping board and smash it with a heavy saucepan, or you can crush it with the side of a wide chopping knife. Sprinkle on a little salt and chop it up until it becomes a gooey pile.

2. Mash the garlic into the butter, if the butter is at room temperature it will be easier. Just keep mashing until it's all combined. You can go ahead and use it like this and it will be great, but if you want to go the extra mile and get the 'wow' factor then squeeze in some fresh lemon juice, about half a lemon's worth, and a handful of fresh, chopped parsley.

3. Slice the bread in 2cm/1 inch thick slices, not cutting all the way through so it stays in one attached piece.

4. Spread the butter onto the slices until it's all used up, you can freeze any remainder or use it on a steak. Wrap the rolls in tinfoil and bake them in a hot oven for 15-20 minutes until crusty, hot and steamy.

Bread Lingo:

Flour types:

Strong White Flour: flour with a higher protein content, making it more suitable for yeast breads.

Plain White Flour: better suited to cakes, scones and soda bread.

Stoneground Wholemeal: mostly unadulterated, nutty brown; for soda breads.

Rye: dark and distinctly tangy, lower-gluten and works well mixed with strong white.

Spelt: a lower-gluten grain, said to be easier on the digestion of sensitive tummies.

Buckwheat: gluten-free, good for pancakes and batters.

Bread lingo:

Sponging the yeast: activating yeast in warm water until it froths.

Kneading: working the dough to develop the gluten structure.

Resting the dough: the time after the bread is kneaded when it doubles in size.

Knocking back: a gentle re-working of the dough, folding it and gently kneading it after resting.

Proving: the final rise of the dough when it's in its shape or tin before baking.

Essential Kit:

A weighing scales: bread baking is quite an exact science, weighing things means better results, a digital one is best. Soda breads are less sensitive to exact measurements.

Measuring spoons: useful for measuring salt, yeast and so on.

Tins: try to find a nice, deep loaf tin to make a nice, deep loaf (alternatively, you can bake loaves in rounds or shape them on a baking tray).

Dough scraper: a small piece of plastic, invaluable for mixing, cutting, portioning, cleaning.

Large plastic bowl: for mixing, resting your dough and so on.

Tea towels: it's good to keep a stash of these specifically for bread baking, to use for covering a dough proving in a bowl, or to use for proving baguettes.

Bibliography

Allen, Darina, *Forgotten Skills of Cooking* (Kyle Cathie Ltd)

Bertinet, Richard, *Dough* (Kyle Cathie Ltd)

David, Elizabeth, *English Bread and Yeast Cookery* (Grub Street)

Ingram, Christine & Shafter, Jenine, *The Complete Book of Bread and Bread Machines* (Hermes House)

Lawson, Nigella, *How to be a Domestic Goddess* (Random House)

Manning, Anneka, *Mastering the Art of Baking* (Murdoch Books)

Ptak, Claire & Dimbleby, Henry, *Leon: Baking and Puddings* (Conran Octopus)

Rhatigan, Prannie, *Irish Seaweed Kitchen* (Booklink)

Ross, Ruth Isabel, *Irish Baking Book* (Gill & Macmillan)

Index

bread bread bread